KIDDIFIED

Don't Kiddify Your Children:
They Are Not Goats

Pastor Cliff McAnthony

Contents

Preface

M any parents have ignorantly Kiddified their children. A Kiddified child is a child that has been turned into a spiritual goat and dedicated to Satan. There are many ways in which parents kiddify their children of which one is calling them kids. In actuality, a kid is a young goat, and many have no idea that "kid" is the name for a young goat. Nevertheless, does it really matter what names we call the children? Is calling the children kids (goats) just a harmless nomenclature? Would a careful biblical examination of this subject lead us to the conclusion that calling children kids is just a harmless nomenclature? Words are powerful and capable of altering the speaker's life and those of the hearers. When God wanted to birth a nation out of Jacob, He reprogrammed Jacob's mindset to create a paradigm shift in how he viewed and treated himself and his family by changing his name from Jacob to Israel. Therefore, from that day onward, Jacob never viewed himself again as just a family, but as one through whom God would raise a nation. The name change created a paradigm shift in Jacob's beliefs, and he saw himself as a nation and not just another family. If this name change which altered Jacob's view of himself and his family had not happened. He and his family would have been swallowed up in Egypt, and there would have been no nation called Israel today. They would have all ended up in Egypt, diffused there, and become Egyptians.

Words are spiritual and powerful enough to create or destroy life. Parents must be discerning, and understand the meaning and spiritual implications of every word they use on their children. Words are spirit and can bring about life or death. John 6:63, *"It is the spirit that quickeneth; the flesh profiteth nothing: the words that I speak unto you, they are spirit, and they are life."* Jesus said that the words he speaks are spirit and life. The opposite side of this will be that the words that Satan speaks, they are spirit and they are death. Therefore, when someone speaks, the words spoken, if inspired by Jesus they will be releasing a life-giving spirit. Also, when someone speaks words inspired by Satan, he or she will be uttering and releasing a death-giving spirit. The idiom: Great or high-sounding name that kills the little dog, is not really talking about dogs, but human beings. The idiom implies that you can destroy a person with external or internal forces by the name you call him or her. If calling children "kids" is inspired by Satan, then we can be certain that it is not just a harmless nomenclature. We can be certain that it invokes the spirit of stubbornness and rebellion in them – the death-giving spirit.

God commanded in the Old Testament that the kid (young goat) be used for the sin offering sacrifice **Numbers 7:22** *"One kid of the goats for a sin offering:"* Satan is the counterfeiter of God's ways. The Satanic world is known for the evil of sacrificing children to Satan. This evil practice of satanic kingdoms is documented in the Bible, Jeremiah 19: 5, *"They have built also the high places of Baal, to burn their sons with fire for burnt offerings unto Baal,..."* This horrific child sacrifice has also been revealed by many ex-satanists/occultic men and women in contemporary times. Satanic men and women have been using children as sacrificial kids (young goats) for thousands of years. Could it be that calling children kids came from these satanic men and women as symbolism for their sacrificial kid (young goat)? Did calling children kids emanate from these evil people because children were their kids (young goats) for sacrifice? Satan is the father goat as revealed in the Scripture and also as symbolized by the image of Satan (Baphomet). Jesus said that all goats will be cast into hellfire with their father Satan on the last day. Is calling our children goats (kids) casting spells on them, dedicating them to Satan, and invoking the death-giving goat spirit into them – the spirit of stubbornness and rebellion? Or is it just a harmless nomenclature to call our children (goats) kids? Have your children been Kiddified? If the mastermind behind calling the children goats is Satan, then you can be certain that it is not just a harmless nomenclature.

Has Satan employed and deployed social media, music, TV, cartoons, video games, dolls, etc as mind-programming agents to kiddify the children? Is he using these devices to lay their foundations to make them conform to his worldviews? Is Satan training them up in the way they should go with these devices so that when they are old they will not depart from it? Proverbs 22:6, *"Train up a child in the way he should go: and when he is old, he will not depart from it."* Has Satan deceived parents into leaving the most valuable period of training their children in his hands through, social media, music, TV, cartoons, video games, and dolls? Has Satan used these devices as kiddifying agents to raise up young kids and big kids for Christian parents? That is to say, young goats and big goats, Kiddified children—children who do not know the LORD nor care about the things of the LORD.

3

Hosea 5:5-7

⁵And the pride of Israel doth testify to his face: therefore, shall Israel and Ephraim fall in their iniquity; Judah also shall fall with them. ⁶They shall go with their flocks and with their herds to seek the LORD; but they shall not find him; he hath withdrawn himself from them. ⁷They have dealt treacherously against the LORD: FOR THEY HAVE BEGOTTEN STRANGE CHILDREN: now shall a month devour them with their portions.

Have Christian parents dealt treacherously against the LORD? Have they begotten strange children: children who do not know the LORD nor care about the things of the LORD?

CHAPTER 1

Call Them Children and Not Kids

Many parents have ignorantly Kiddified their children. A Kiddified child is a child that has been turned into a spiritual goat and dedicated to Satan. There are many ways in which parents kiddify their children. One of which is calling their children kids. Many people in contemporary times especially in the Western world call children "kids". The media, movies, and songs echo this. It is acceptable across all spheres of life to call children kids. The secular world, the church, and parents are all on board in calling children kids. Most people and parents in the Western world call children kids except for a few with understanding. In actuality, a kid is a young goat and many have no idea that kid is the name for a young goat. Nonetheless, does it really matter what names we call the children? Is calling the children kids (goats) just a harmless nomenclature? Would a careful biblical examination of calling children kids lead us to the conclusion that it is a harmless nomenclature? Have your children been Kiddified? Let us carefully examine the pages of the Scripture and see what it says on this subject matter.

1.1 The Power of Spoken Words

Words are powerful and capable of altering the speaker's life and those of the hearers. The words that proceed from a person's mouth will reveal his or her person. Your words are your personhood, you cannot be separated from your words. You are the same person with your spoken or written words. This is why you could get sued or even killed for the words you spoke or wrote because your word is you and you will be held accountable for your words.

Matthew 12:36-37

³⁶But I say unto you, that every idle word that men shall speak, they shall give account thereof in the day of judgment. ³⁷For by thy words thou shalt be justified, and by thy words thou shalt be condemned.

John 1:1-3

¹In the beginning was the Word, and the Word was with God, and the Word was God. ²The same was in the beginning with God. ³All things were made by him; and without him was not anything made that was made.

John 3:1-3 clearly reveals that a person is not different from his or her word. The passage shows that God is the same with His Word. The Scripture personifies the Word of God and says that all things were made by the Word of God and that the Word of God is God. This means that the words that proceeded from the mouth of God in the beginning to create all things was the same as God which is Jesus Christ the Word made flesh.

Genesis 1:1-3;31

¹In the beginning God created the heaven and the earth. ²And the earth was without form, and void; and darkness was upon the face of the deep. And the Spirit of God moved upon the face of the waters. ³And God said, let there be light: and there was light. [31]And God saw everything that he had made, and, behold, it was very good. And the evening and the morning were the sixth day.

Words are spiritual and very powerful and could be used to create or destroy life. The creation account (Genesis 1:1-31) reveals that God spoke everything into existence by the Words of His mouth which is also Him. This gives us a glimpse of the power of the spoken word. This is not particular to God alone it also pertains to humans because God created man in His own image and likeness.

Genesis 1:26-27

[26]And God said, let us make man in our image, after our likeness: and let them have dominion over the fish of the sea, and over the fowl of the air, and over the cattle, and over all the earth, and over every creeping thing that creepeth upon the earth. [27]So God created man in his own image, in the image of God created he him; male and female created he them.

Throughout the Scripture are numerous examples of men of God exercising the power of the spoken word to speak life or destruction into existence. One example of this as it relates to children is the story of prophet Elisha and the children of the city.

2Kings 2:25-24

[23]And he went up from thence unto Bethel: and as he was going up by the way, there came forth little children out of the city, and mocked him, and said unto him, go up,

thou bald head; go up, thou bald head. ²⁴And he turned back, and looked on them, and cursed them in the name of the LORD. And there came forth two she bears out of the wood, and tare forty and two children of them.

It was only at Prophet Elisha's spoken word that these bears came out of the wood and destroyed these 42 children. This is why parents must be very careful in cursing or name-calling their children. Permit me to tell you a true story about a daughter and her mother. It happened that the daughter was obstinate and would not obey or respect the mother at all times. So, a day came that she put up one of her obstinate behaviors which I may not remember exactly now but out of provocations the mother laid a curse on her by saying these words; " for this thing you have done, you will suffer before you give birth to any child, you will suffer so as to know the pains I went through to have you and you have the right to this". It was just casual but the power in her spoken words resonated years later after the daughter got married, while in the labor room. The story had it that this young lady labored for days and while in the hospital, pastors were invited to come and pray for her but to no avail. As doctors were confused as to why the baby wouldn't come out despite the full dilation and smooth process, the Holy Spirit reminded her of her mother's words years back and she requested that her mother be sort for immediately. People were asking what would her mother do in a situation like this when she is not a medical professional. As soon as the mother arrived, the daughter began to ask for forgiveness but the mother was ignorant of the past ordeal as the daughter narrated. However, she queued in immediately and began to reverse all her spoken words following her daughter's confession. While she was broken and still speaking with deep emotions, the baby came forth and people became speechless while learning their lesson. Just imagine that the mother was no more, what do you think would have happened? Probably she would have died or lost the child.

In the same line was a story of a man in my village whose father cursed for raising his hand against him. The father cursed him out of annoyance, the father said, "For this act, you shall never set your eyes on me again." As the son returned back to his base in Cameroon, he died and never set his eyes on his father again. Words are powerful tools that must be used wisely by parents. Therefore, parents who want to raise godly children for the LORD must desist from cursing their children. They must be very discerning, and understand the meaning and spiritual implications of every word they use on their children. Words are spirit and can bring about life or death. John 6:63, *"It is the spirit that quickeneth; the flesh profiteth nothing: the words that I speak unto you, they are spirit, and they are life."* Jesus said that the words he speaks are spirit and life. The opposite side of this will be that the words that Satan speak, they are spirit and they are death. Therefore, when someone speaks; the words spoken, if inspired by Jesus they will be releasing a life-giving spirit. Also, when someone speaks words inspired by Satan, he or she will be uttering and releasing a death-giving spirit. One of the words frivolously used by parents on their children in contemporary times is "kid". In actuality, kid means young goat, and your child is not a goat. If calling children kids is inspired by Satan, then we can be certain that it is not just a harmless nomenclature. We can be certain that it invokes the spirit of stubbornness and rebellion in the children – the death-giving spirit.

Genesis 37:31, And they took Joseph's coat, and killed a kid of the goats, and dipped the coat in the blood;

Genesis 38:17, And he said, I will send thee a kid from the flock. And she said, wilt thou give me a pledge, till thou send it?

Numbers 7:16, One kid of the goats for a sin offering:

Isaiah 11:6, The wolf also shall dwell with the lamb, and the leopard shall lie down with the kid; and the calf and the young lion and the fatling together; and a little child shall lead them.

Above are just a few Scriptures that tell us what a kid is in the Bible. The dictionary also made this clear that a kid is a young goat. Isaiah 11:6 talks about the future millennial reign of Jesus Christ and the peace and safety that would be attained. How wild and ferocious beasts such wolf, leopard, and lion would live in peace with domestic animal like lamb, kid and calf and a little child will take care of them. This verse clearly shows that the creator made a clear distinction between a kid and a child. God calls human offsprings children, and not kids (goats). Proverbs 22:6 says, Train up your CHILD, not your KID (GOAT). Why do you call them goats and expect them to behave like children? The question you should ask is, why did the world invent the idea of calling children "kids" and why not lambs? It is because God called His own Lamb and Satan must create the opposite. John 1:36, *"And looking upon Jesus as he walked, he saith, Behold the Lamb of God!"*

This clearly reveals the mastermind behind this kid-calling invention. It is in the DNA of Satan to try to change whatever God says and does to the very opposite; to call good evil and evil good. God created two genders, male and female. Satan and his agents are saying that there are multiplicities of genders and you can change your gender to any imaginary gender of your choice from hell. They also deny that man was created by God in His own image. They claim that man evolved from other animals which had their long evolutionary journey from rocks after a big bang that took place billions of years ago. It is Satan's character to try to change whatever God says to the very opposite. Satan is the mastermind behind calling good, evil, and evil, good. God called the offspring of man, children, and Satan has deceived humanity to change it into goats (kids). Jesus called his children sheep and Satan has deceived humanity to call their own goats (kids). Is calling children goats (kids) just a harmless nomenclature? If the mastermind behind calling the children goats is Satan, then you can be certain that it is not just a harmless nomenclature. If calling the children kids was inspired by Satan, then you can be sure that it invokes a death-giving spirit in them. Words are spirit and are able to bring about life or death. John 6:63, *"It is the spirit that quickeneth; the flesh profiteth nothing: the words that I speak unto you, they are spirit, and they are life."* Jesus said that the words he speaks are spirit and life. The opposite side of this will be that the words that Satan speak, they are spirit and they are death. Therefore, when someone speaks words inspired by Satan, he or she will be uttering and releasing a death-giving spirit. A Kid is the Satanic informal way of addressing a child. Therefore, do not turn your children into spiritual goats through your spoken words. If kid calling was inspired by Satan, then they must be releasing a death-giving spirit when uttered. Parents who want to train godly children should desist from calling their children kids. Call them children, and not kids (goats).

1.2 The Effects of Names on Bearers

Someone may ask, does it matter if I call them children or kids (goats)? Have you ever heard of the saying: "If you want to kill a dog, give it a bad name?" Nothing has changed in the dog's character; it is the same good dog. But if you want to kill it, just give it a bad name. That means the name will influence how people see, react, or respond to that dog. If you see a good dog coming and start saying, this mad dog is coming, people will either run or go on the offensive and attack the dog to protect themselves. The dog is not mad, but calling it a mad dog automatically changes how people respond to it. No matter how good a dog is, if you give it a bad name, people will view and relate to it according to that name. This is just one aspect of name-calling.

Have you also heard of this idiom: Great or high-sounding name that kills the little dog? These idioms are not really talking about dogs, but human beings. The idioms are simply saying that you can destroy a person with external or internal forces by the name you call him or her. In the first idiom, the name destroys the bearer from outsiders. People respond or deal with that person based on the influence of what they have heard about the person. In the second case, "great or high-sounding name that kills the little dog:" this name affects the dog itself and destroys it from within. The dog is given a high-sounding name that makes it feel it is something greater than it really is. A great or high-sounding name will pomp pride in a person and cause him or her to want to carry himself/herself to measure up with that high-sounding name. Some of us grew up answering various kinds of nicknames. For example, Superman, Iron Man, Hulk Hogan, and Spiderman, to name a few. Did those names not stir us up to want to act like those names' characters? Certainly yes, names are highly influential and affect us from within or from without. In Mark 3:17, Jesus nicknamed James and his brother John "Boanerges," which means The Sons of Thunder, and in Luke 9:51-56, we see them trying to live up to that name.

Mark 3:17

And James the son of Zebedee, and John the brother of James; and he surnamed them Boanerges, which is, The sons of thunder:

Luke 9:51-56

⁵¹And it came to pass, when the time was come that he should be received up, he steadfastly set his face to go to Jerusalem, ⁵²And sent messengers before his face: and they went, and entered into a village of the Samaritans, to make ready for him. ⁵³And they did not receive him, because his face was as though he would go to Jerusalem. ⁵⁴And when his disciples James and John saw this, they said, Lord, wilt thou that we command fire to come down from heaven, and consume them, even as Elias did? ⁵⁵But he turned, and rebuked them, and said, Ye know not what manner of spirit ye are of. ⁵⁶For the Son of man is not come to destroy men's lives, but to save them. And they went to another village.

Satan also understands this principle, and since his goal had always been to eradicate godliness and destroy Christianity. He knew to start from the foundation; our children, and to start with the basics of changing their names. Just like God changed the name of Jacob to Israel. He changed their names from children to goats (kids). Let us look at some of the Satanic Ten-points Agenda by Alice A. Bailey for the New World Order and understand how the devil has been working in the past years.

1. Take God and prayer out of the education system. If people grow up without reference to God, they will consider God irrelevant to daily life. (In the last fifty years, this has happened. God is irrelevant to most people.)

2. Reduce parental authority over children. Break communication between parents and children so the parents can't pass on spiritual values to their children. Do this by pushing excessive child rights.

3. Destroy the traditional Christian family structure. Break the traditional Judeo-Christian family concept.

4. If sex is free, make abortion legal and easy. Remove restrictions on sex. Sex is the biggest Joy, and Christianity robs people of this. People must be freed to enjoy it without restrictions.

From the few points mentioned above, we can clearly see that the devil's primary target is our children. Most of these plans were implemented more than fifty years ago. Many who were raised within that age group in the Western world don't want anything to do with God, because they were raised as goats (kids). Goats are stubborn and rebellious; they have the character of witchcraft because rebellion is like the sin of witchcraft. The spiritual reality is that goats – the Kiddified, (Those with goatlike character) have no place in the kingdom of God.

1Samuel 15:23

For rebellion is as the sin of witchcraft, and stubbornness is as iniquity and idolatry. Because thou hast rejected the word of the LORD, he hath also rejected thee from being king.

I emphasize name-calling because it is a significant aspect of child training that parents must consider if they want to succeed in correcting their children's character. Now remember that the point here is not so much the name itself, but the source and purpose for the name. God wants to create a paradigm shift with this knowledge about calling our children goats in order to realign our thoughts and beliefs with His Word on how we view and deal with our children. The realignment of thought and mind that will cause parents to train their children adequately in the ways of the LORD.

Genesis 32:28

And he said, thy name shall be called no more Jacob, but Israel: for as a prince hast thou power with God and with men, and hast prevailed.

God changed Jacob's name to Israel as seen in the above Scripture. Why did God change Jacob's name? Was it just that Jacob did not sound right or there was a bigger picture to it?

Certainly, there was a bigger picture to it. Despite changing Jacob's name, when God appeared to Moses in the burning bush centuries later, He still referred to Himself as the God, of Abraham, Isaac, and Jacob. Also, when Jesus spoke to the Sadducees on the resurrection of the dead, He referred to God as the God of Abraham, Isaac, and Jacob. Why is God still calling him Jacob despite changing his name to Israel?

Exodus 3:6

Moreover, he said, I am the God of thy father, the God of Abraham, the God of Isaac, and the God of Jacob. And Moses hid his face; for he was afraid to look upon God.

Matthew 22:31-32

[31]But as touching the resurrection of the dead, have ye not read that which was spoken unto you by God, saying, [32]I am the God of Abraham, and the God of Isaac, and the God of Jacob? God is not the God of the dead, but of the living.

Jesus still referred to God as the God of Jacob. Why not the God of Israel? It is because it was not really about the name, but the reprogramming of Jacob's mind to create a paradigm shift in how he views and treats himself and his family. God wanted to achieve a reprogramming of Jacob's mindset to birth a nation. Therefore, from that day onward, Jacob never viewed himself again as just a family, but as one through whom God would raise a nation. The name change created a paradigm shift in Jacob's beliefs, and he saw himself as a nation and not just another family. If this name change which altered Jacob's view of himself and his family had not happened. He and his family would have been swallowed up in Egypt, and there would have been no nation called Israel today. They would have all ended up in Egypt, diffused there, and become Egyptians.

But because God had created in them the mindset that they were not just a family, but a nation of their own. They went into Egypt believing they were a nation called Israel and would surely come out of Egypt to their own land. Let us have a glimpse of their transformed mindset in the words of Jacob himself and his son Joseph, as seen below.

Genesis 48:21

And Israel said unto Joseph, Behold, I die: but God shall be with you, and bring you again unto the land of your fathers.

Genesis 50:24-25

[24]And Joseph said unto his brethren, I die: and God will surely visit you, and bring you out of this land unto the land which he swore to Abraham, to Isaac, and to Jacob. [25]And Joseph took an oath of the children of Israel, saying, God will surely visit you, and ye shall carry up my bones from hence.

God visited Jacob and created in him a paradigm shift in belief, which he passed down to his sons so they would not lose their identity. They almost faced extermination in Egypt at the cruel hands of Pharoah, but they had hope in God to keep His promise. Eventually, He rescued them, and the nation of Israel was born the day they left Egypt to go to their own land as God had promised their forefathers.

1.3 Satan's Deception on Youths to Call Themselves Dogs

What did the Bible say about dogs? Biblical perspective on the nature and character of dogs is negative and God will never call His children dogs. He will not be pleased with His children calling themselves dogs or manifesting the characteristics of a dog. This is not to say that dogs are not good animals or that God hates dogs. On the contrary, God said that everything He created is very good, and this includes dogs. What we are talking about here is spiritual and relates to the character of dogs. God detests any human being that manifests the nature and character of a dog. Here are some Bible verses that express God's position on the nature and characteristics of dogs.

Proverbs 26:11, As a dog returneth to his vomit, so a fool returneth to his folly.

Matthew 7:6, Give not that which is holy unto the dogs, neither cast ye your pearls before swine, lest they trample them under their feet, and turn again and rend you.

Matthew 15:26, But he answered and said, it is not meet to take the children's bread, and to cast it to dogs.

Philippians 3:2, Beware of dogs, beware of evil workers, beware of the concision.

Revelation 22:15, For without are dogs, and sorcerers, and whoremongers, and murderers, and idolaters, and whosoever loveth and maketh a lie.

The Scriptures above reveal that God detests those that manifest the nature and characteristics of dogs and that they have no place in His kingdom. However, Satan has rewritten all that negativity in our time through music. We can see this, especially in the hip-hop music world, where young people happily proclaim and celebrate that they are dogs. Satan inspired rap music artists to use doggy stage names like Doggy Fresh, Snoop Dogg, Dog Pound, Lil Bow Wow, Pitbull, etc. He went further to inspire them and other music artists who do not have such names to glorify the nature and pleasure of the doggy lifestyle. Dogs and their nature and character are now glamorized and glorified. They and their followers openly proclaim that they are dogs, they put on dog chains and doggy pendants of all kinds. They glamorize the nature and characters of dogs and take pleasure in behaving like dogs. The same nature and character which God hates and says that those of such nature have no place in His Kingdom.

Revelation 22:15:

For without are dogs, and sorcerers, and whoremongers, and murderers, and idolaters, and whosoever loveth and maketh a lie.

Through music, Satan sent out demonic spirits to infest the human mind and body to manifest the characteristics of dogs in man. And what does this do in the lives of these singers and their listeners/fans? The more they confess that they are dogs, the more they invoke the demonic doggy spirit in them, taking them deeper and deeper into sin. Thereby alienating them further away from God and aligning them with hell and Satan. We must understand that name-calling is very important. When people profess themselves to be dogs, these demonic spirits take over them and begin to produce and manifest those doggy characters they glorify. This is one of the reasons you see so much sexual promiscuity and violence among these dog-glamorizing hip-hop artists and their fans. They find it normal and entertaining to engage in reckless sexual lifestyles with multiple partners. They unashamedly glamorize and glorify their doggy lifestyles. This is one of the reasons why there is so much promiscuity and violence in the hip-hop community, after all, dogs sleep around and fight each other "Dog eat Dog". They are just doing the doggy things because doggy demonic spirits have taken over them and are manifesting themselves through them.

1.4 How Did Humanity Arrive at Calling Their Children Goats (Kids)?

A kid is the young of a goat. God commanded in the Old Testament that the kid (young goat) be used for sin offering sacrifices. The children of Israel sacrificed kids (young goats) before the LORD as an offering for their sins as documented in the Old Testament.

Leviticus 23:19

Then ye shall sacrifice one kid of the goats for a sin offering, and two lambs of the first year for a sacrifice of peace offerings.

Numbers 7:21-22

[21]One young bullock, one ram, one lamb of the first year, for a burnt offering: [22]One kid of the goats for a sin offering:

Satan is a counterfeiter of God's ways. The devil counterfeited this sacrifice, replacing the kid with a child, and requested child sacrifice from his worshippers. The Satanic world is known for the evil of sacrificing children to Satan. This evil of child sacrifice has been practiced for thousands of years by evil men and women in their idolatrous worship of Satan. This horrific practice spanned across all the continents of the world, from Europe among the Druids to South and Central America, to Asia, and Africa.

This horrific practice of satanic kingdoms is documented in the Bible and has been revealed by many ex-Satanists/ occultic men and women in contemporary times. I recommend you watch Joseph Okechukwu's videos *"Shadows of Darkness Part 1, 2 & 3"* on rumble to get a glimpse of what these evil satanic men and women do with children in secret.

Jeremiah 19:4-5; 32:35

⁴Because they have forsaken me, and have estranged this place, and have burned incense in it unto other gods, whom neither they nor their fathers have known, nor the kings of Judah, and have filled this place with the blood of innocents; ⁵They have built also the high places of Baal, to burn their sons with fire for burnt offerings unto Baal, which I commanded not, nor spake it, neither came it into my mind:

³⁵And they built the high places of Baal, which are in the valley of the son of Hinnom, to cause their sons and their daughters to pass through the fire unto Molech; which I commanded them not, neither came it into my mind, that they should do this abomination, to cause Judah to sin.

The above Bible verses in Jeremiah and many others revealed the evil practice of child sacrifices by Satanists. God is saying that they have built altars to Baal and offered their sons as burnt offerings to Baal. The phrase *"to cause their sons and their daughters to pass through the fire unto Molech;"* in Jeremiah 32:35 does not mean that the children went through the fire and are alive on the other end. Molech is a god, the god of the Ammonites, and is a spirit. To pass through the fire unto Molech means to go through the fire into the spirit world to be with Molech. This means that the children were horrifically offered to Molech by burning them alive in the fire. The children entered the fire alive, died, and entered the spirit world to be with Molech. This understanding is in consonant with what God said earlier in Jeremiah 19: 5, *"They have built also the high places of Baal, to burn their sons with fire for burnt offerings unto Baal,..."* Satanic men and women have been using children as sacrificial kids (young goats) for thousands of years. Could it be that calling children kids came from these satanic men and women in contemporary times as symbolism for their sacrificial kid (young goat)? Did calling children kids emanate from these evil people because children were their kids (young goats) for sacrifice? Satan is the father goat as revealed in the Scripture and also as symbolized by the image of Satan (Baphomet). Jesus said that all goats will be cast into hellfire with their father Satan on the last day.

Matthew 25:32-34,41

[32] And before him shall be gathered all nations: and he shall separate them one from another, as a shepherd divideth his sheep from the goats: [33] And he shall set the sheep on his right hand, but the goats on the left. [34] Then shall the

King say unto them on his right hand, Come, ye blessed of my Father, inherit the kingdom prepared for you from the foundation of the world: ⁴¹Then shall he say also unto them on the left hand, Depart from me, ye cursed, into everlasting fire, prepared for the devil and his angels:

Speaking of the last day in the passage above, Jesus said He will gather all nations and separate them into two categories; the sheep and the goats. The sheep He will put on His right hand and the goats on His left. The sheep on His right hand are blessed and are His, and He will bring them into His Kingdom. But the goats on His left are cursed and are Satan's, and He will cast them into everlasting fire (hellfire) to be with the devil for eternity. This Bible passage shows that goats are the children of the devil and will eventually end up in hellfire for eternity with their father Satan. If goats are the children of Satan, then calling children goats (kids) could not have been inspired by God. The name goat (kid) is the opposite of what God called His children. Surely, calling children goats is inspired by Satan the father of all goats. And he has used his kiddifying agents like music, social media, TV, cartoons, and celebrities to promote and glamorize calling children kids (goats). Could calling our children goats (kids) be casting spells on them, dedicating them to Satan, and invoking the death-giving goat spirit into them, the spirit of stubbornness and rebellion? Or is it just a harmless nomenclature to call our children (goats) kids? Have your children been Kiddified? That is to say, turned into spiritual goats and dedicated to Satan.

1.5 Unmasking How Calling Children "Kids" Stimulates Negative Behaviors

When you call your children "kids" (goats); it is not just a nice way of calling them goats. Unknown to you over time, your perception will be conditioned spiritually to view them as goats. In other words, you will not see anything wrong with them manifesting the stubborn and rebellious characters of goats. You will not see it necessary to train them to desist from such characters. You will assume it to be their nature and okay for them to behave that way. Your mindset would be to leave them alone because they are just kids (goats). They will become goats to you spiritually, and consequently, you will treat them as such (Not train them appropriately). On the other hand, you will continually dedicate them to Satan by invoking the death-giving goat spirit into them as you call them kids (goats). They will eventually become Kiddified and grow up to become "big kids (big goats)" that is, adult goats.

Matthew 25:33-34, 41

[33]And he shall set the SHEEP ON HIS RIGHT HAND, but the GOATS ON THE LEFT. [34]Then shall the King say unto them on his right hand, Come, ye blessed of my Father, inherit the kingdom prepared for you from the foundation of the world: [41]Then shall he say also unto them on the LEFT HAND, Depart from me, ye cursed, into everlasting fire, prepared for the devil and his angels:

I believe you now understand that it is the devil who came up with the idea that parents should call their children goats (kids). You can clearly see that this is the devil's character of countering whatever God says or does with the very opposite like he is doing with marriage, creation, gender, etc. Jesus called His children sheep and called the devil's children goats. Then the devil used satanic men and women, entertainment industries, the media, and social media and enticed parents to start calling their children goats (kids). Why did the world not call them lamb if it is just a harmless name? It is because the devil is in the details, he is the spirit behind calling children kids. The devil is the spirit that is behind opposing whatever God says or does. The devil is the one behind calling evil good and good evil; putting darkness for light and light for darkness; calling sweet bitter and bitter sweet. He deceives humanity to do so because he knows that God's damnation awaits those who do such.

Isaiah 5:20

Woe unto them that call evil good, and good evil; that put darkness for light, and light for darkness; that put bitter for sweet, and sweet for bitter!

Have you ever wondered why the devil's image of Baphomet is that of a goat? Yes, the devil is the father goat and has manipulated parents to cast spells and dedicate their children to him by calling them baby goats (kids). Calling your children kids (goats) cast spells on them, and dedicate them to the devil. It invokes the death-giving goat spirit into them – the spirit of stubbornness and rebellion, which is the spirit of the devil. The devil knows that goats will burn with him in hell for all of eternity. That is why he deceived parents to raise their children like goats so that on the last day, they would hear what Jesus said in Matthew 25:33,41, *³³And he shall set the sheep on his right hand, but the GOATS ON THE LEFT. ⁴¹Then shall he say also unto them on the left hand, Depart from me, ye cursed, into everlasting fire, prepared for the devil and his angels:*

Jesus says we should bring our children to Him. Unfortunately, many parents have made their children goats spiritually and are laboring hard to bring goats to Jesus. Goats cannot come to Jesus; they are stubborn and rebellious like their father the devil. If you can be honest with yourself, you would have observed these two characters in your children that you have unknowingly labeled as goats. Jesus says we should bring our children to Him and not goats. He said that the Kingdom of God is for children and not goats. Therefore, do not alienate your children from the kingdom of God by dedicating them continually to Satan and invoking the hell-bound death-giving goat spirit into them by calling them kids (goats).

Luke 18:16

But Jesus called them unto him, and said, Suffer little children to come unto me, and forbid them not: for of such is the kingdom of God.

However, it is not really the name kid by itself that condemns children to the ungodly goat's behaviors of stubbornness and rebellion. Rather, it is the subtle reprogramming or retraining of the minds of parents in a way that has caused a paradigm shift in how they think and relate to their children. Your children are not necessarily behaving like goats simply because you are calling them goats (kids). You could still call them children and still treat them as goats and they will behave like goats. Children are born in a fallen state because man fell from glory in the Garden of Eden. Therefore, children are born with innate mischief or foolishness.

Proverbs 22:15

Foolishness is bound in the heart of a child; but the rod of correction shall drive it far from him.

The devil's goal was to produce a paradigm shift in belief on how people view and relate to their children by selling this idea of calling children kids (goats) to parents. This kid (goat) calling became prominent in the 1840s and was glamorized in the early sixties and seventies. Christians, especially in America, withstood it for a while but later gave in. Unfortunately, the devil succeeded in his goal to create a paradigm shift in how parents view and relate to their children. If you have ever been around real kids, that is the young of goats, you will perfectly understand what took place. Baby goats just jump around playfully until they become adult goats. They do not need any training; they just jump around playfully until they grow to become stubborn adult goats.

Satan aimed to subtly work on parents and children psychologically to produce his desired results. He created a paradigm shift in belief and understanding of how parents should deal with their children. So instead of training them appropriately, they will excuse their ungodly stubborn characters and say "They are just kids (goats). Instead of disciplining them promptly when they are misbehaving, they excuse their bad behaviors and say "They are just kids (goats)" Why? Because parents have been conditioned in their minds to think of them as kids (goats), and the children are being destroyed. Calling children kids (goats) affects parents

27

internally by changing their understanding and perspective on training their children. Then it affects the children externally by the way parents train their children because of their goat (kid)-skewed perspective of their children. Then it affects the children internally as they observe their parents ignore and condone some of their bad behaviors. Making them believe that they are just kids (goats) and that it is okay for them to act mischievous and stubborn. Therefore, they grow up believing their bad characters are normal and acceptable. Their parents allowed them to stray because they were conditioned by Satan to see their offspring as goats (kids).

I traveled to North Dakota in 2021 for a revival program we organized, and after the church service on Sunday, we came out for coffee and snacks. While we stood in the queue for coffee and snacks, some of our children just noisily ran to the front and were about to start grabbing snacks. I rebuked them and asked them to be orderly and do the right thing by joining the queue. Then one sister said: "Let them be; they are just kids." But I objected, telling her and the children that they were not kids but children and had to follow the same principles of life, behave orderly, and join the queue to be served. Then the sister sarcastically said to me okay, Mr. Daddy. The children gladly joined the queue and got their snacks and drinks. From this story, you can clearly see the kid-skewed view of that sister and how it was affecting the children. She sees it okay for the children to behave rowdy and disorderly because they are just kids (goats). She finds it needless to train them and sees their behaviors as acceptable because they are just kids (goats). The children felt it was acceptable for them to be rowdy and disorderly because they knew that people viewed them as just kids (goats) and that it was perfectly okay for them to behave that way.

Kids or goats are not meant to be trained. So, they playfully jump around and kid around until they become big kids (goats). That is why you hear people say "I am just kidding around", yes that is what real kids (young goats) do, they kid around. The Bible says to train up a child, not a kid. Goats are born and allowed to jump around playfully until they become adult goats. Calling children kids is just programming them to become spiritual goats who will not receive training or discipline. They grow bodily but remain the same in their character. You might have heard parents or adults say of a child, "He is just a big kid." Unknowingly to them, they are simply saying, he is just a big goat, (he wasn't trained).

What God achieved in Jacob and his family by changing Jacob's name to Israel is what Satan achieved in most parents and children today. When parents call their children goats (kids) they create a wrong identity of their children in their minds and that of their children. "Oh, they are just kids (goats) "some parents say, allowing their children to go unpunished, unsupervised, untrained, and wayward. The power of confession; you often get what you profess with your mouth Num 14:28, *"Say unto them, as truly as I live, saith the LORD, as ye have spoken in mine ears, so will I do to you:"* Therefore, confess positively, speak right things, and rightly call your offsprings, children.

You could still call your offspring children. But in your mind, you still see them as goats and consequently treat them as such. Therefore, the most important thing is not changing what you call them, but deprogramming your mind from the "Just a kid (goat)" mentality. Then reprogram your mind to see them as the children that the LORD called them and position your heart to train them. Proverbs 22:6 *"Train up a child in the way he should go: and when he is old, he will not depart from it."* PLEASE CALL YOUR GOD-GIVEN OFFSPRING CHILDREN AND NOT GOATS.

CHAPTER 2

Start Training at Ground-Zero (Age 0)

S tart training your child at age zero. Training must begin at Ground-zero, in the foundational stage of character molding (ages 0-7) to be most effective and lasting. Most parents do not start training their children from age zero. They presume that they are too small or not cognitive enough to learn. This is just ignorance on the part of the parents. When the Bible says: *"Train up a child in the way he should go: and when he is old, he will not depart from it."* The child there refers to children from ages 0-7. King Josiah was raised by his mother to fear and obey the Lord within this age period. He became king at age eight as a godly child and never departed from the way of the LORD all the days of his life.

2Kings 22:1-2

¹Josiah was eight years old when he began to reign, and he reigned thirty and one years in Jerusalem. And his mother's name was Jedidah, the daughter of Adaiah of Boscath. ²And he did that which was right in the sight of the LORD, and walked in all the way of David his father, and turned not aside to the right hand or to the left.

2.1 The Intellect of A Child

Most parents do not really understand how intelligent a child is. They often view the child from an adult perspective, how much knowledge they have about things, and their level of reasoning. Then they conclude that the child is just ignorant. Yes, they are correct that the child is ignorant. However, ignorance does not mean the child is unintelligent or cognitively impaired, it just means the child doesn't know much. Obviously, the child does not know much, he just arrived in a new world and must pay good attention to observe and to learn various skills in order to adapt to his new world. Just imagine yourself as an adult suddenly disappearing from this known world and finding yourself in an alien world. You will be confused and ignorant of all that is going on there. The aliens will also view you as just ignorant. However, this will not mean that you are unintelligent or cognitively impaired. It just means that you don't know much and need much data (knowledge) and time to understand things and adapt to your new world. Now, you are in this alien world, you do not understand their language and most things going on there. In this condition all you will give attention to is learning; observing and processing everything you see to gain some understanding. Imagine how much more you would learn things properly if any alien would be kind enough to sacrifice time to give you attention to teach you things and proper decorum. This is the condition the newborn finds his or herself in. Though he or she does not know much (ignorant), he/she is not unintelligent or cognitively impaired. The child is eager to observe and learn. All the child needs is an adult who will be kind enough to give him or her attention and teach him/her decorum and godliness.

Early years psychology says, "Give me the child until he is seven years old, and I will make him what you want him to be." This psychology says ages zero to seven are a child's formative years;

character molding-wise. Everything else we do to mold a child's character after they turn seven cannot be foundational and may not last. The philosophy is, "The earlier, the better."

The early years psychology says a child's formative years are from zero to seven years. Anything after that cannot be foundational and will likely not last. And this is where many Christian parents fail. They neglect training their children in their formative years, thinking that their children are too young to be taught the things of God or the principles of life. Then when the children grow up astray, they start blaming the children and often abuse them in their effort to correct them.

When I was back home in Nigeria, at a point in time I lived with an uncle who later traveled abroad for greener pastures. I was then living with his wife and newly born daughter. I noticed that his wife was very lenient with their daughter to a fault. When their daughter started crawling, I observed that her mother removed all the ceramic decorations or breakable things in the living room. She removed anything in the living room that she thought her daughter could break or destroy.

I often corrected her and advised her to teach her daughter to adapt to her environment and make her daughter understand what to touch and what not to touch. But she always says that her daughter was just a child. I was busy most days and did not spend much time at home. But when I did, I made sure I trained this little girl. If she crawls to the TV or to any other property that is not right for her to play with and touches it. I would gently spank her little fingers and change the countenance on my face. Then she would look at my face and of course, it wasn't pleasant, then she would start crying. This continued for a while, and with time, she understood her boundaries, at least whenever I was at home. She was able to learn at about seven months when she was still crawling that there are boundaries in life. She was smart enough to learn that there are things she should not do, and places she should not go. If I happened to be in the living room and she crawled to the TV or to any other place I had forbidden her, or that she is not sure whether she is allowed to go to or touch. She would stop, turn, and look at me to see the expression on my face. If I changed my countenance to a frown, she would understand that she is not supposed to touch it or crawl further. She will immediately change direction and move on to something else. But if I smile at her, she will smile back and continue with her intended business.

The little girl learned discipline and to reverence me from the gentle redirection and training that I gave her at that tender age. By the time she was six years old, having been under my discipline and training, she learned to obey me in everything. Whenever I ask her to stop or sit down; she knows to do so immediately. She took my every instruction seriously. But for her mother, she had no reverence for her. Before her mother could finish giving her an instruction, she would object with NO! Then her mother would pounce on her with her hands in anger, forgetting that she did not train her correctly in the first place. She had trained her daughter not to fear or reverence her and taught her that there are no boundaries in life without saying a word. She trained her daughter to be stubborn and rebellious to her without intending to do so. She Kiddified her daughter without calling her kid (goat). This stresses the fact that you could still kiddify a child without calling them a kid (goat). Whenever parents view their child from the perspective that he or she is just a child; as an excuse for not disciplining them early and promptly. It is the same with he or she is just a kid (goat) mentality. The only difference is that they did not refer to the child as a kid (goat). Nonetheless, their mentality is still the same goat-like skewed perspective that the child is too young to be trained. Whenever parents fail to train their children appropriately at the foundational stage. They have unknowingly succeeded in training them to be stubborn and rebellious. They have created a vacuum for the death-giving goat spirit to enter their children – the spirit of stubbornness and rebellion. The parents themselves have become a tool in the hands of Satan to kiddify their children.

Now that her daughter has grown to be six years old without any foundational training from her. She was now trying to set boundaries and exercise authority over her daughter. Her actions left her daughter confused instead of learning anything. The girl knew there were no boundaries with her all along growing up and her thought would be how come mom is acting like this now? How come she is now saying you cannot do this or that? This is why she was rebellious to her mom. Her mom wanted to reap what she did not sow in her. She wasted her opportunity to train her daughter and discipline her during the foundational years claiming she was just a child. Unknowingly to her, she was a kiddifying agent in the hands of Satan for the kiddification of her daughter.

Children are intelligent and smart, even from a very tender age. Take, for example, a child who is still breastfeeding. Most often, when they start developing their first teeth, their mother's nipples are in trouble. If the child bites her nipple and she claim he is just a child, the child will keep biting. However, the child will remember not to do it again if the mother corrects him with a gentle smack a few times. The child will quickly learn that biting mom while sucking is not an acceptable behavior. Children from zero to seven do not know much, they are ignorant, nevertheless, they are intelligent. They are like empty containers that will accept whatever their parents pour into them. Therefore, pour godly training into their lives and leave no vacuum for Satan to kiddify them.

Training must begin at Ground-Zero at the foundational stage of ages 0 – 7 to be most effective and lasting. Early years psychology says, "Give me the child until he is seven and I will make him what you want him to be." This psychology says ages zero to seven are the formative years of a child's life; that is, character molding-wise. Everything else parents do after ages 0 – 7 to mold the character of a child cannot be foundational and may not last. The philosophy is, "The earlier the better." This is secular psychology. The world and Satan understand this God-given natural principle and take due advantage of it. Proverbs 22:6 ***"Train up a child in the way he should go: and when he is old, he will not depart from it."***

2.2 Satan's Strategies to Lay Your Children's Foundation

Unfortunately, while Christians treat the Word of God with levity, Satan does not. Satan believes the Word of God and he is fully aware that not one jot or title of God's Word will go unfulfilled. Satan understands that the Word of God is effective and eternal.

Matthew 5:18

For verily I say unto you, till heaven and earth pass, one jot or one title shall in no wise pass from the law, till all be fulfilled.

Satan knows that the Word of God is true and forever settled in heaven. **Psalm 119:89 "Forever, O LORD, thy word is settled in heaven."** Satan knows that God's Word cannot fail and that every biblical principle is true and effective. He knows that the foundation of the entire existence of the world and life hangs and thrives on God's Word.

Hebrews 1:1-3

[1]God, who at sundry times and in divers manners spake in time past unto the fathers by the prophets, [2]Hath in these last days spoken unto us by his Son, whom he hath appointed heir of all things, by whom also he made the worlds; [3]Who being the brightness of his glory, and the express image of his person, and UPHOLDING ALL THINGS BY THE WORD OF HIS POWER, when he had by himself purged our sins, sat down on the right hand of the Majesty on high;

Hebrews 11:3

Through faith we UNDERSTAND THAT THE WORLDS WERE FRAMED BY THE WORD OF GOD, so that things which are seen were not made of things which do appear.

God upholds all things He created by the Word of His power. The foundation of the world and life are formed and sustained by the invisible Word of God. Godliness in a family, society, nation, and holy Christian living starts at the foundation of life. Satan knows this and for the reason to stop godliness and destroy Christianity in the world. He knew well to start from the foundation by hindering parents from raising godly children. The Satanic Ten Points Agenda to destroy Christianity and usher in a new world order by the infamous Satanist Alice A. Bailey started with the children. This agenda was given by Satan to destroy the Christian Worldview and create a paradigm shift in belief and lifestyle that will eventually usher in the reign of the Anti-Christ.

ALICE A BAILEY'S TEN POINTS AGENDA FOR NEW WORLD ORDER

1. TAKE GOD AND PRAYER OUT OF THE EDUCATION SYSTEM

2. REDUCE PARENTAL AUTHORITY OVER THE CHILDREN

3. DESTROY THE JUDEO-CHRISTIAN FAMILY STRUCTURE OR THE TRADITIONAL CHRISTIAN FAMILY STRUCTURE

4. IF SEX IS FREE, THEN MAKE ABORTION LEGAL AND MAKE IT EASY

5. MAKE DIVORCE EASY AND LEGAL, FREE PEOPLE FROM THE CONCEPT OF MARRIAGE FOR LIFE

6. MAKE HOMOSEXUALITY AN ALTERNATIVE LIFESTYLE

7. DEBASE ART, MAKE IT RUN MAD

8. USE MEDIA TO PROMOTE AND CHANGE MINDSETS

9. CREATE AN INTER-FAITH MOVEMENT

10. GET GOVERNMENTS TO MAKE ALL THESE LAWS AND GET THE CHURCH TO ENDORSE THESE CHANGES.

Take God and Prayer Out of the Education System

The first point is to remove God and prayer from the education system. This is primarily targeted at children. Alice Bailey explains that if people grow up without reference to God, they will consider God irrelevant in their day-to-day lives. Satan knew that he could not succeed with his agenda to overthrow Christianity, that is godliness and usher in the New World Order of life as long as the children were being taught the Word of God and prayers in schools. The children will grow up with some knowledge of God's Word and the fear of God and will learn to believe and trust God; which will form the foundation of their life; character molding-wise. Therefore, Satan strategized to subtly remove God's Word and prayer from the foundational stage of their life and replace them with secular and anti-God knowledge. Satan knows that the children will not depart from his desired lifestyle if he succeeds in shaping them in knowledge and character at the foundational stage –Ground-Zero, (ages 0–7). Everything else people do to mold the character of children after ages zero to seven cannot be foundational and may not last. The philosophy is, "The earlier the better." The world and Satan understand this God-given natural principle and take due advantage of it. Proverbs 22:6 *"Train up a child in the way he should go: and when he is old, he will not depart from it."*

Why is Satan desperately after the children? Because he knows that if he could capture the children, then he would have captured the human race. He knows children will not depart from the godless foundation he would have laid in their lives. Alice Bailey said, "If the people grew up without reference to God. Then they will consider God irrelevant in their day-to-day life." Has Satan succeeded? If you carefully observe most people born within the last fifty years in first-world countries like the United States, Canada, Australia Europe, and so on, you will see that this has happened. God has become irrelevant in most people's day-to-day life. The most unfortunate thing is that it is almost impossible to get people who grew up with this marred and corrupted foundation to ever consider God in the true sense of Christianity. Even when they do, at some point they are most likely to fall back and align with the foundation that was already laid in their life. Only through special divine mercy and intervention from the Almighty God will one ever see a different outcome. The above statement may be hard to accept now, however, understanding will come as you read on; let's move forward.

Reduce Parental Authority Over the Children.

Alice Bailey further explained; "Break communication between parents and children so that parents cannot pass on spiritual values to their children. Do this by pushing excessive child rights." If you live in the Western world; you would perfectly understand this and know how and why children got to be given unprecedented rights over their parents by the government. The agenda behind those excessive child rights in most of the Western world is to break the communication between parents and children. Satan achieves this by weakening and destroying parental authority over their children by enacting excessive child rights and laws. The child is then programmed like a robot with these child rights starting from their daycare. The child is thought to report their parents to the school authority for emotional abuse anytime their parents yell at them, or rebuke/scold them. And to call the police for physical abuse if they are flogged or feel threatened by their parents. Satan is the brain behind it all because he wants to have your children at the foundational stage, ages 0 –7 so that he can lay the foundation of their lives unchallenged with everything secular and anti-God.

Satan knows that the foundation determines the outcome of the structure. "Give me the child until he is seven and I will make him what you want him to be." Everything else done after ages zero to seven to mold the character of the child cannot be foundational and may not last. "The earlier the better." This is secular psychology. The world and Satan understand this God-given natural principle and take due advantage of it. Proverbs 22:6 ***"Train up a child in the way he should go: and when he is old, he will not depart from it."*** Satan knows that God's Word cannot fail and that every biblical principle is true and effective. Therefore, he exploits this biblical truth and principles to establish his evil agenda. While Christians continue to trivialize the same Word of God that was so powerful to bring man and the entire creation into being and to sustain them.

2.3 The Significance of Life's Foundation

The foundation of a building is what determines and sustains the structure to be erected. The foundation determines the weight, size, and design that can be erected. It is the primary power source of resistance for any structure. Structures built on faulty or marred foundations cannot withstand the opposing forces of the natural elements. Errors made at any level of construction are easier to correct so that they align with the foundation laid. However, if the foundation is faulty, it simply means that the structure cannot stand and to correct it is to bring down the entire structure and the foundation to start all over. Failure or refusal to do so will not change the outcome but multiply the damages as the structure will eventually collapse on its own destroying lives and other properties. The foundation takes priority in construction and is the most important part of the building process because it is on it that everything else stands. It will be a futile effort to lay a weak foundation for a bungalow while laboring to build a skyscraper on it. The foundation laid, determines the capacity and shape/design of the structure that could be erected and the power of its resistance against unfriendly natural and manmade adversities. Jesus spoke about the significance of a good solid foundation.

Luke 6:48-49

[48]He is like a man which built an house, and digged deep, and laid the foundation on a rock: and when the flood arose, the stream beat vehemently upon that house, and could not shake it: for it was founded upon a rock. [49]But he that heareth, and doeth not, is like a man that without

a foundation built an house upon the earth; against which the stream did beat vehemently, and immediately it fell; and the ruin of that house was great.

In the same vein as a parent, you are building a house (life) that is of eternal value and far more important than a structure of bricks and wood. Proverbs 22:6 *"Train up a child in the way he should go: and when he is old, he will not depart from it."* To train up is to build the child's life. You will have to dig deep into that child's life and lay his or her foundation on the solid Rock which is Jesus – God's Word. Your efforts to build your child's life and raise a godly child will be futile if you are building on a weak, marred (corrupted), or wrong foundation. That is, a foundation laid upon the wrong or corrupted gospel, philosophies of men, false religion, secularism, and anti-God knowledge. This is the reason why the Lord said: *If the foundations be destroyed, what can the righteous do?* Psalms 11:3. I believe by now you can understand why I made this statement earlier; *"The most unfortunate thing is that it is almost impossible to get people who grew up with this marred and corrupted foundation to ever consider God in the true sense of Christianity. Even when they do, at some point, they are most likely to fall back and align with the foundation that was already laid"* God said it Himself, that the efforts of the righteous be it of the preacher, the parents or the child is futile if the foundation is destroyed. Psalms 11:3 *"If the foundations be destroyed, what can the righteous do?"* Now can you understand the significance of a child's foundation? Therefore, you must labor hard as parents, paying and paying whatever costs and sacrifices necessary to lay a solid foundation for your children. That is, a foundation built on the truth of God's Word.

It is of utmost importance that you give it all to lay a good solid foundation for your children because the great thing about it is that they will not be able to depart from it. Proverbs 22:6 ***"Train up a child in the way he should go: and when he is old, he will not depart from it."*** If you succeed in digging deep to lay the foundation of your child's life on the truth of the gospel, and not on another gospel. Even if the child deviates through external influences from relatives, schools, friends, and social media as he or she grows up. However, because a foundation has been laid already every wrong structure erected on it will not fit in and will eventually collapse. Think of it this way you are building a house and you laid a foundation for a rectangular structure and someone else comes and starts to build a circular structure on it. It will not fit in and when he realizes himself, he will destroy the wrong structure and follow the pattern of the foundation that was laid. If he does not stop and continues with the wrong structure, it is only a matter of time before the entire thing will collapse and he will start afresh to build the right structure in compliance with the foundation already laid. This was the case in the story of the prodigal son.

Luke 15:11-19

[11]And he said, a certain man had two sons: [12]And the younger of them said to his father, Father, give me the portion of goods that falleth to me. And he divided unto them his living. [13]And not many days after the younger son gathered all together, and took his journey into a far country, and there wasted his substance with riotous living. [14]And when he had spent all, there arose a mighty famine in that land; and he began to be in want. [15]And he

went and joined himself to a citizen of that country; and he sent him into his fields to feed swine. ¹⁶And he would fain have filled his belly with the husks that the swine did eat: and no man gave unto him. ¹⁷And when he came to himself, he said, How many hired servants of my father's have bread enough and to spare, and I perish with hunger! ¹⁸I will arise and go to my father, and will say unto him, Father, I have sinned against heaven, and before thee, ¹⁹And am no more worthy to be called thy son: make me as one of thy hired servants.

The prodigal son did not stop building the wrong structure until the whole thing collapsed. He was able to come to himself and realize that the life he is living now does not fit into the foundation of his life and he said I will arise and return to my father, that is, return to my foundation and start to build afresh, Hallelujah! Glory to God Almighty. *Luke 15:17-19: And when he came to himself, he said, How many hired servants of my father's have bread enough and to spare, and I perish with hunger! I will arise and go to my father, and will say unto him, Father, I have sinned against heaven, and before thee, And am no more worthy to be called thy son: make me as one of thy hired servants.* Imagine if he had no such foundation, he would not have been able to have any standard of measurement to compare his present life's condition to understand that he is off course. He would have seen his present life's condition as normal and would have continued to build on it to his final doom.

2.4 The Impact of King Josiah and King Joash's Early Childhood Upbringing

There is a great difference in how King Josiah and King Joash were raised at the foundational stage of their upbringing – the character formative stage of ages zero to seven. Their upbringing played a decisive role in the outcome of their life. Proverbs 22:6 *"Train up a child in the way he should go: and when he is old, he will not depart from it."*

King Josiah's Early Childhood Upbringing

King Josiah was raised by his mother and received godly training that formed the foundation of his life which he could not depart from all his life. He was raised to fear and obey the LORD within the foundational stage of ages zero to seven. He became king at age eight as a godly child and never departed from the way of the Lord all the days of his life.

2Kings 22:1-2

¹Josiah was eight years old when he began to reign, and he reigned thirty and one years in Jerusalem. And his mother's name was Jedidah, the daughter of Adaiah of Boscath. ²And he did that which was right in the sight of the LORD, and walked in all the way of David his father, and turned not aside to the right hand or to the left.

King Josiah was trained to be a God-fearing child by his mother Jedidah. Probably that is why the mother's name was referenced instead of the father to show who was responsible for the outcome of King Josiah's character. We can also see similar references in the Bible for Pastor Timothy and King Ahaziah who did evil.

2Timothy 1:5; 3:14-15

1:5When I call to remembrance the unfeigned (genuine) faith that is in thee, which dwelt first in thy grandmother Lois, and thy mother Eunice; and I am persuaded that in thee also. 3:14But continue thou in the things which thou hast learned and hast been assured of, knowing of whom thou hast learned them; 3:15And that from a child thou hast known the holy scriptures, which are able to make thee wise unto salvation through faith which is in Christ Jesus.

Timothy's grandmother Lois, and mother Eunice were referenced as the people who influenced and trained Timothy to be established in the faith. What made Timothy steadfast in the faith and stand out from the corruption and moral decline that plagued the ministers and believers in his days is made clear in 2 Timothy 3:15 *"And that from a child thou hast known the holy scriptures, which are able to make thee wise unto salvation through faith which is in Christ Jesus."* He was taught the faith from childhood (age 0-7) by his grandmother and mother. They laid a solid godly foundation that he could not depart from all the days of his life.

2Chronicles 22:2-4

2Forty and two years old was Ahaziah when he began to reign, and he reigned one year in Jerusalem. His mother's name also was Athaliah the daughter of Omri. 3He also walked in the ways of the house of Ahab: for his mother was his counsellor to do wickedly. 4Wherefore he did evil in the sight of the LORD like the house of Ahab: for they were his counsellors after the death of his father to his destruction.

King Ahaziah's mother Athaliah was referenced as the one who schooled him in evil and sustained him with counsel on how to prosper in evil. A child will always follow and build on the foundation laid in his or her life whether good or evil. Athaliah laid a solid evil foundation for her son Ahaziah which he could not depart from all the days of his life. Parents, please sacrifice all that is necessary to lay a godly foundation for your children. You will never regret it. Your sacrifice will bless your life, and family, and bless humanity. King Josiah's mother must have sacrificed so much to ensure that Josiah was raised a God-fearing young man. It was all within the ages of zero to seven – the foundational stage in child training. He never departed from that foundation all the days of his life.

2Kings 22:1-2

¹Josiah was eight years old when he began to reign, and he reigned thirty and one years in Jerusalem. And his mother's name was Jedidah, the daughter of Adaiah of Boscath. ²And he did that which was right in the sight of the LORD, and walked in all the way of David his father, and turned not aside to the right hand or to the left.

King Josiah grew up with his mother who did not give him away to nannies and daycares to waste his foundational age of character molding. She sacrificed time and resources to teach and train her son. She did not allow another to lay a wrong foundation in his life, she protected him and laid the godly foundation she desired to see in his life. She got what she desired and labored for in works and prayers. It is said that "money corrupts, and power corrupts absolutely," but not King Josiah. Although he had both money and power; and must have faced great temptations to do wickedly at a very young age. Yet he failed not, because his mother had laid a solid godly foundation in his life. King Josiah never departed from the godly foundation his mother laid all the days of his life. Proverbs 22:6 *"Train up a child in the way he should go: and when he is old, he will not depart from it."* Glory to God Almighty who is able to keep that which is committed into His hand.

King Joash's Early Childhood Upbringing

In contrast to King Josiah's early childhood upbringing, King Joash did not have a godly mother or father to train him. King Joash was nursed up and not trained. He was given to a nurse at his foundational stage of ages zero to seven to nurse him up, that is, to raise him just like you would raise chickens. The nurse was there to feed and nourish him, it does not require training but to ensure he is well fed, kept healthy, clean and happy.

2Chronicles 22:10-12

¹⁰But when Athaliah the mother of Ahaziah saw that her son was dead, she arose and destroyed all the seed royal of the house of Judah. ¹¹But Jehoshabeath, the daughter of the king, took Joash the son of Ahaziah, and stole him from among the king's sons that were slain, and put him and his nurse in a bedchamber. So Jehoshabeath, the daughter of king Jehoram, the wife of Jehoiada the priest, (for she was the sister of Ahaziah,) hid him from Athaliah, so that she slew him not. ¹²And he was with them hid in the house of God six years: and Athaliah reigned over the land.

Jehoshabeath the sister to King Ahaziah hid Joash from Athaliah his grandmother to save his life. She hid him in a room and assigned someone to nurse him up for six years. Joash must have been one year old when he was given to the nurse. He was seven years old when he was made the king of Judah after being nursed for six years. Picture the scenario, a nurse was paid wages to raise the son of a king. Do you think she would dare to discipline or even rebuke him for fear? No, I don't think so, she would not want to lose her job or risk getting punished. She only performed her duties as a nurse and not as a mother. She did not train King Joash, he was a child left to himself.

Proverbs 29:15

The rod and reproof give wisdom: but a child left to himself bringeth his mother to shame.

A child left to himself does not mean that there was no adult in his life. It means that the rod of correction and reproof was not employed in his or her upbringing. The child was not disciplined promptly with the rod of correction; and reproofed at his wrongdoings. King Joash's foundational years were spent feeding him and ensuring he was healthy and happy. He had no godly parent to train him in the way of the LORD like the case of King Josiah. How did this come to affect him adversely? He deviated from following the LORD at his later age after all the godly training he received from Jehoiada the priest. He could only follow the LORD and do right while Jehoiada was alive. But as soon as Jehoiada died he destroyed all the godly structures that Jehoiada had erected on his life's faulty foundation and started to build evil structures that fit the foundation that was laid in his life by Satan.

2Chronicles 24:2,17-22

²And Joash did that which was right in the sight of the LORD all the days of Jehoiada the priest. ¹⁷Now after the death of Jehoiada came the princes of Judah, and made obeisance to the king. Then the king hearkened unto them. ¹⁸And they left the house of the LORD God of their fathers, and served groves and idols: and wrath came upon Judah and Jerusalem for this their trespass. ¹⁹Yet he sent prophets to them, to bring them again unto the LORD; and they testified against them: but they would not give ear. ²⁰And the Spirit of God came upon Zechariah the son of Jehoiada the priest, which stood above the people, and said unto them, Thus saith God, Why transgress ye the commandments of the LORD, that ye cannot prosper? because ye have forsaken the LORD, he hath also forsaken you. ²¹And they conspired against him, and stoned him with stones at the commandment of the king in the court of the house of the LORD. ²²Thus Joash the king remembered not the kindness which Jehoiada his father had done to him, but slew his son. And when he died, he said, The LORD look upon it, and require it.

This is why the LORD said in Psalms 11:3, *"If the foundations be destroyed, what can the righteous do?"* All the efforts made by Jehoiada the priest to raise King Joash a godly man were in vain. King Joash's foundation was marred and corrupted by Satan because he was a child left to himself. The rod of correction and reproof was not employed in his childhood upbringing. He was not disciplined promptly with the rod of correction; and reproofed at his wrongdoings. Satan used the nurse assigned to Joash to kiddify him. The death-giving goat-like spirit of stubbornness and rebellion filled the void left in his life due to the lack of godly training. Therefore, as soon as Jehoiada died he rebelled and turned aside to align himself with the foundation that Satan laid in his life.

Sadly, this is the case for many children, especially of those in the Western world and of rich parents no matter their geographic location. These parents neglect the foundational stage of their children's upbringing because they are too busy chasing after wealth, power, and fame or simply because they are ignorant. They employ nannies and daycares; and pay them their wages to waste and lay whatever foundation they deem fit in their children's lives just like in the case of King Joash.

These parents often devote time to ensure their children get the best nourishment and comfort in life. They take them to the best restaurant to eat, buy them the best electronic gadgets, and provide them luxury bedrooms furnished with TVs and computers. They take them to the best hospitals and ensure regular checkups and good food supplements. They send them to the best schools and employ private lesson teachers. They take them to the best resorts around the world for vacations to ensure they enjoy all the good pleasures of life and are happy.

Christian parents should never raise their children like this. Children raised by nannies and daycares are usually children left to themselves. They will never grow up with the godly foundation of their parents if they have any. The nannies and daycares are only there for their wages and Satan will use them to lay an ungodly foundation in the lives of your children. Some of these nannies and daycares are Satan's kiddifying agents. Some of them might be witches and witchhouses. They will surely get your children Kiddified. Christian parents should emulate Jedidah King Josiah's mother, Timothy's grandmother Lois, and mother Eunice in early childhood upbringing. They sacrificed time and resources to labor in training and prayers to raise godly children. Your sacrifices, labor, and prayers will never be in vain, because the Almighty God watches over His Word to perform it, and He said *"Train up a child in the way he should go: and when he is old, he will not depart from it."* Proverbs 22:6. Your sincere godly efforts and sacrifices in early childhood training will eventually bless your life, your family, and humanity. Their lives will bless generations to come just like those of King Josiah and Pastor Timothy; because God watches over His Word to perform it.

2.5 Ground-Zero Godly Training Shields from Peer Pressure and Bad Role Model Influence

There may be no established protection strategies that parents could use to protect their children from external influence and pollution of peer pressure and negative role models. Nevertheless, when a child is given proper godly training from Ground-Zero it will shield him or her from external negative influences. When a solid godly foundation is laid within the foundational character molding years of ages zero to seven. It will form a formidable shield to protect and keep that child from peer pressure and the influence of all negative role models. A good biblical example is that of the child Samuel.

1Samuel 1:20-22

[20]Wherefore it came to pass, when the time was come about after Hannah had conceived, that she bare a son, and called his name Samuel, saying, Because I have asked

him of the LORD ²¹And the man Elkanah, and all his house, went up to offer unto the LORD the yearly sacrifice, and his vow. ²²But Hannah went not up; for she said unto her husband, I will not go up until the child be weaned, and then I will bring him, that he may appear before the LORD, and there abide for ever.

Hannah being barren earnestly sought the Lord in prayers for a male child and promised to give the child back to God. God answered her prayers and she gave birth to Samuel who became a great prophet in Israel. After the birth of Samuel, Hannah said to her husband that she would not take the child to the house of God yet until he was weaned. 1Samuel 1:22 *"But Hannah went not up; for she said unto her husband, I will not go up until the child be weaned, and then I will bring him, that he may appear before the LORD, and there abide for ever."* She wanted to wean the child knowing that he would not be coming back home again once he got there. Wean, means to cause a child to cease from elementary dependency on the mother for breast milk and Activities of Daily Living (ADLs), and to cease from childish habits. In other words, this means to train up a child. Hannah knew that she needed to perform her duty of training up her child before giving him to the LORD as she promised.

Hannah did not just wean Samuel from dependency on breast milk and Activities for Daily Living (ADLs) but weaned him from the dependency on carnal food. She fed him with spiritual food – the Word of God and taught him to depend on spiritual food. Luke 4:4 *"And Jesus answered him, saying, it is written, That man shall not live by bread alone, but by every word of God."* This was what Hannah taught her child

Samuel. She trained him to depend on the Word of God. The age at which Samuel was brought to the House of God and handed over to Eli the priest was not specified. How much is known, is that he was brought to the House of the LORD after he was weaned. The right age for weaning in humans ends around seven years. This is evidenced in the Bible with King Josiah and King Joash. They were not made kings until they were weaned. Therefore, one can safely say that Samuel was brought to the house of the Lord at a young age between seven and eight. 1Samuel 1:24. *"And when she had weaned him, she took him up with her, with three bullocks, and one ephah of flour, and a bottle of wine, and brought him unto the house of the LORD in Shiloh: and the child was young."*

The second aspect of weaning a child is to train the child to cease from childish habits. 1Corinthians 13:11, *"When I was a child, I spake as a child, I understood as a child, I thought as a child: but when I became a man, I put away childish things."* Childish characters are ungodly because man is born in a sinful state inherited from Adam. That is why you do not have to teach a child how to lie, steal, be greedy, selfish, and manipulate with crying to have his way, etc. The child's natural inclination is to be disorderly, and sinful, and to love the world and the things of the world. 1John 2: 15-16, *"Love not the world, neither the things that are in the world. If any man love the world, the love of the Father is not in him. For all that is in the world, the lust of the flesh, and the lust of the eyes, and the pride of life, is not of the Father, but is of the world."* It takes training to teach a child decorum and to get him to fear and love God. Hannah knew that a child left to himself (without training) would cause grief Proverbs 29:15, *"The rod and reproof give wisdom: but a child left to himself bringeth his mother to shame."* She did not want to give the LORD a child that would cause shame. She sacrificed all that was necessary to train up a godly child. She denied herself traveling with her husband to the House of the LORD to devote time to raising a godly child for the LORD. King David said he would not give God that which cost him nothing, 2Samuel 24:24. You cannot raise a godly child for the LORD without paying the price for it. Hannah paid the price and she succeeded. The solid godly foundation she laid in Samuel within the foundational stage (character molding ages, 0 –7) paid off in preserving him from external influence of peer pressure and ungodly role models.

1Ssamuel 2:12,17,18,22

[12]Now the sons of Eli were sons of Belial; they knew not the LORD. [17]Wherefore the sin of the young men was very great before the LORD: for men abhorred the offering of the LORD. [18]But Samuel ministered before the LORD, being a child, girded with a linen ephod. [22]Now Eli was very old, and heard all that his sons did unto all Israel; and how they lay with the women that assembled at the door of the tabernacle of the congregation.

Samuel did not learn to fear and love God in Eli's house because Eli and his wife failed to raise godly children for the LORD. They could not train their children in the fear of God. It is obvious that they could not have been the ones responsible for the godly outcome of Samuel's life. The fear and the love of God in Samuel were imparted to him at home by his mother

Hannah. Eli the priest and his wife failed God in their duty of raising godly children for the LORD. They could not sacrifice time and resources to train up their children in the fear of God and they were severely judged and punished by God 1Samuel 2:27-36. The Bible says that his sons were the sons of Belial, that is, sons of Satan. They did not know God and were evil in their character. They were greedy and sexually immoral, and these were the people that Samuel lived in the same house with as he grew up. They were Samuel's peers and role models being his seniors and yet could not corrupt him.

Who else would have had the greatest influence on a young man growing up besides his peers and elder brothers who are often his immediate role models? Eli's sons were elder brothers and immediate role models for Samuel; he did not follow their evil ways despite being far away from his mother. Satan knew that God had called Samuel to be a great prophet in Israel to restore Justice and righteousness. One could only imagine the peer pressure and temptations that Satan would have daily hurled at Samuel through Eli's sons and others. Nevertheless, he did not give in to peer pressure and evil influence. This was only possible because a solid godly foundation had been laid in his life by his mother. The godly training Hannah gave Samuel in his foundational years (ages 0 to 7) shielded him from all external influences of peer pressure and negative role models. Samuel did not depart from the godly training he received from his mother. Proverbs 22:6 *"Train up a child in the way he should go: and when he is old, he will not depart from it."* Samuel grew up to become a great prophet in Israel with great honor. He never practiced the injustice, greed, and sexual immorality of Eli's sons. He restored justice and righteousness to the people of God, lived a righteous life, and ended his ministry in righteousness.

1Samuel 12:1-5

¹And Samuel said unto all Israel, Behold, I have hearkened unto your voice in all that ye said unto me, and have made a king over you. ²And now, behold, the king walketh before you: and I am old and grayheaded; and, behold, my sons are with you: and I have walked before you from my childhood unto this day. ³Behold, here I am: witness against me before the LORD, and before his anointed: whose ox have I taken? or whose ass have I taken? or whom have I defrauded? whom have I oppressed? or of whose hand have I received any bribe to blind mine eyes therewith? and I will restore it you. ⁴And they said, Thou hast not defrauded us, nor oppressed us, neither hast thou taken ought of any man's hand. ⁵And he said unto them, The LORD is witness against you, and his anointed is witness this day, that ye have not found ought in my hand. And they answered, He is witness.

This is what foundational (early childhood) godly training can produce in a child's life. Glory to God Almighty who watches over His Word to perform them for those who obey Him. God watched over His Word Proverbs 22:6, ***"Train up a child in the way he should go: and when he is old, he will not depart from it."*** and performed it in Samuel's life for Hannah because she believed it and did her part to train Samuel. God will likewise do the same for you; if only you would believe His Word and do your part to sacrifice all that is needed to train your child in the way of the LORD.

2.6 The Crucial Role of Mothers in Ground-Zero Child Training

Mothers play a critical role in child training; their role is decisive in the outcome of a child's life. The role of mothers in child training determines the future of the child. This is so because the foundational stage in character molding is between ages zero to seven and at this stage, the child is closest to the mother. Between ages zero to seven the child is dependent on the mother for breast milk and ADLs. The child sees the mother as the primary caregiver and looks up to her for food, ADLs, and training. There are also times when men find themselves in this role because of unfortunate circumstances like the death or illness of the mother, because of divorce, or children out of wedlock. It could also be because of socioeconomic status where the mother is the breadwinner of the home which may hinder her from playing her motherly role effectively. It could also be as a result of the dysfunctional contemporary world where mothers simply neglect their God-given role in child training. Whatever the case may be, the parent who is in the motherly role at the character molding stage of ages zero to seven should know that he or she is playing a decisive role in the child's life. This period of a child's life should never be taken for granted. Nevertheless, the focus here is on the mother to whom God has naturally assigned this role due to her unique qualities and disposition.

Women are naturally the primary caregivers of the child during the character-molding stage. The infant child from day one depends on the mother for food, warmth, and love which the child receives from suckling. These essential needs provided by the mother naturally create a bond between the child and the mother on day one. This makes the mother the closest person to the child from day one, and training must begin at Ground-Zero to be most effective and lasting. Early years psychology says, "Give me the child until he is seven and I will make him what you want him to be." This psychology says ages 0–7 are the formative years of a child; character molding-wise. Everything else we do after ages 0–7 to mold the character of the child cannot be foundational and may not last. The philosophy is, "The earlier the better." Proverbs 22:6 *"Train up a child in the way he should go: and when he is old, he will not depart from it."*

Mothers play a unique critical role in child training due to their natural disposition. Their role determines the child's future. This character formative years can be likened to "garbage in, garbage out." You will always receive returns with interest on whatever you put in as training whether good or bad. If you put in nothing because you are so busy with mundane things. Know that that there are no vacuums in life and this also applies to your children. Satan will help you to ensure that your child is filled with garbage and Kiddified through his various agents. Throughout the Scripture, mothers have shaped the future of their children through their training whether for good or for evil.

King Ahaziah: 2Chronicles 22:2-4

²Forty and two years old was Ahaziah when he began to reign, and he reigned one year in Jerusalem. His mother's name also was Athaliah the daughter of Omri. ³He also walked in the ways of the house of Ahab: for his mother was his counsellor to do wickedly. ⁴Wherefore he did evil in the sight of the LORD like the house of Ahab: for they were his counsellors after the death of his father to his destruction.

King Ahaziah became an evil king in Judah who did wickedly against the Lord, and the full credit for the outcome of his life was given to his mother Athaliah. The mother did not suddenly become his counselor after he was crowned king as an adult. His mother being his counselor shows that the mother schooled him in evil right from his character formative years and now that he is old, he cannot depart from evil. The foundation laid in King Ahaziah's life by his mother at Ground-Zero is evil. Therefore, as the king has nothing else to offer but evil, who then should be his counselor? Those who are experts at doing evil, and who else is more qualified in Judah as an evil expert than Athaliah his mother? Do you now see why his mother became his counselor? The role of a mother in the outcome of a child's life cannot be overemphasized.

King Amon: 2kings 21:19-22

[19]Amon was twenty and two years old when he began to reign, and he reigned two years in Jerusalem. And his mother's name was Meshullemeth, the daughter of Haruz of Jotbah. [20]And he did that which was evil in the sight of the LORD, as his father Manasseh did. [21]And he walked in all the way that his father walked in, and served the idols that his father served, and worshipped them:[22]And he forsook the LORD God of his fathers, and walked not in the way of the LORD.

King Amon reigned as an evil king and his mother is mentioned for us to know who trained him. We must remember that God does not use words carelessly when studying the Scripture. Every word mentioned in the Bible is of great necessity to understanding the message and what took place. Amon's father was King Manasseh who also did evil in the sight of God and was also trained by his mother Hephzibah. 2Kings 21:1-2,18 *"Manasseh was twelve years old when he began to reign, and reigned fifty and five years in Jerusalem. And his mother's name was Hephzibah. ²And he did that which was evil in the sight of the LORD, after the abominations of the heathen, whom the LORD cast out before the children of Israel. ¹⁸And Manasseh slept with his fathers, and was buried in the garden of his own house, in the garden of Uzza: and Amon his son reigned in his stead."*

Amon's father was a king and obviously would not have the time to provide nursing care and ground-zero training for his son. Moreover, in those days it was traditional for women to play their natural role in early childhood care and training. He walked in all the ways of his father, does not mean that his father laid that foundation. 2Kings 2:20-21 *"And he did that which was evil in the sight of the LORD, as his father Manasseh did. And he walked in all the way that his father walked in, and served the idols that his father served, and worshipped them:"* Most likely King Manasseh would not have had time to spend with Amon at his foundational stage, ages 0-7. It just shows that his father was also an evil king and he chose to follow his father's ways. King Amon's outcome in life may have been different if he had a godly mother who laid a godly foundation in his life. This truth can be seen in the case of King Josiah his son who had a godly mother that laid a godly foundation in her son's life.

King Josiah: 2Kings 22:1-2

¹Josiah was eight years old when he began to reign, and he reigned thirty and one years in Jerusalem. And his mother's name was Jedidah, the daughter of Adaiah of Boscath. ²And he did that which was right in the sight of the LORD, and walked in all the way of David his father, and turned not aside to the right hand or to the left.

Josiah became king at age eight and did that which was right in the sight of the Lord all the days of his life. Amazingly, King Amon who did evil like his father King Manasseh was the father of King Josiah. Nonetheless, King Josiah did not turn out to do evil like his father King Amon. Rather, he walked in the way of his father David. King David is King Josiah's grandfather of many generations. King Josiah never knew King David in person, it was just to show that King Josiah chose to walk in the ways of King David as seen in the case of King Amon who chose to walk in the way of his father King Manasseh. The outcome of King Josiah's life was different from that of his father King Amon though they both had evil fathers. The godly outcome of King Josiah's life was different because he had a godly mother who did a great job in training him to become a godly child like his father David. The Ground-Zero godly child training his mother Jedidah laid formed the bedrock of King Josiah's character. This godly foundation enabled King Josiah to choose to do that which was right in the sight of the LORD all the days of his life. King Josaiah's mother's role in his ground-zero training, that is, early childhood training is clearly revealed in 2Kings 22:1, *"Josiah was eight years old when he began to reign, and he reigned thirty and one years in Jerusalem. And his mother's name was Jedidah, the daughter of Adaiah of Boscath."* Again, we can clearly see that the outcome of King Josiah's life was fully credited to his mother. "Give me the child until he is seven and I will make him what you want him to be." Who was with Josiah from ages zero to seven? His mother Jedidah. She did not fail in her duty and the Word of God came true for her. Proverbs 22:6 *"Train up a child in the way he should go: and when he is old, he will not depart from it."* Many mothers fail to adequately play this critical role in their children's lives and when the inevitable ungodly outcome begins to manifest, then they start to fast and pray. This is not to say that you should not fast and pray in such a situation. But sacrificing time and resources to train your child, especially in their foundational stage – ages 0-7 is far more important, effective, and rewarding than any corrective measure one may take in the future.

King Jehoahaz 2Kings 23:29-32

²⁹In his days Pharaohnechoh king of Egypt went up against the king of Assyria to the river Euphrates: and king Josiah went against him; and he slew him at Megiddo, when he had seen him. ³⁰And his servants carried him in a chariot dead from Megiddo, and brought him to Jerusalem, and buried him in his own sepulchre. And the people of the land took Jehoahaz the son of Josiah, and anointed him, and made him king in his father's stead. ³¹Jehoahaz was twenty and three years old when he began to reign; and he reigned three months in Jerusalem. And his mother's name was Hamutal, the daughter of Jeremiah of Libnah. ³²And he did that which was evil in the sight of the LORD, according to all that his fathers had done.

King Jehoahaz was the son of King Josiah, a godly man who served God faithfully all the days of his life. How then did his son turn out to be an evil person? It is crucial to pay good attention to this storyline. King Josiah had an evil father, King Amon and yet he did not turn out to become an evil person. Then on the other hand King Josiah's son King Jehoahaz turned out to become evil despite having a father as godly as King Josiah. Jehoahaz became evil because he had a mother who did not sacrifice time and pleasure to train him in the way of the LORD at his foundational stage. His mother Hamutal was mentioned to let us know the person responsible for his upbringing during his foundational stage of ages zero to seven. King Josiah turned out a godly person despite having an evil father King Amon because he had a godly mother who sacrificed time and pleasure to train him in the way of the LORD at his foundational stage. Mothers play a critical, and decisive role in the outcome of a child's character. The role of mothers in child training determines the future character of the child. This is so because the child is closest to the mother and dependent on her for everything at the foundational stage in character molding. What mothers do or fail to do to mold the child's character at this stage will ultimately decide whether the child will become good or evil.

King Lemuel: Proverbs 31:1-5

[1]The words of king Lemuel, the prophecy that his mother taught him. [2]What, my son? and what, the son of my womb? and what, the son of my vows? [3]Give not thy

strength unto women, nor thy ways to that which destroyeth kings. ⁴It is not for kings, O Lemuel, it is not for kings to drink wine; nor for princes strong drink: ⁵Lest they drink, and forget the law, and pervert the judgment of any of the afflicted.

These are the words of King Lemuel, obviously he was a good king as reflected in his words in Proverbs Chapter 31. Who taught him to do right as revealed in the Scripture? his mother. Proverbs 31:1 *"The words of King Lemuel, the prophecy that his mother taught him."* The full credit for the outcome of King Lemuel's life was again given to his mother. His mother taught him that women, wine, and strong drinks destroy destiny. She sang it like a song to Lemuel until it was engraved on the foundation of his life. He did not depart from his mother's teachings because they were laid at the foundational stage of his life. The life and words of King Lemuel as taught him by his mother are still blessing humanity today. Proverbs 22:6 *"Train up a child in the way he should go: and when he is old, he will not depart from it."*

Prophet Samuel: 1Samuel 1:20-22; 12:1,3-5

²²But Hannah went not up; for she said unto her husband, I will not go up until the child be weaned, and then I will bring him, that he may appear before the LORD, and there abide for ever. ¹And Samuel said unto all Israel, Behold, I have hearkened unto your voice in all that ye said unto me, and have made a king over you. ³Behold, here I am: witness against me before the LORD, and before his anointed: whose ox have I taken? or whose ass have I taken? or whom have I defrauded? whom have I oppressed? or of whose hand have I received any bribe to blind mine eyes therewith? and I will restore it you. ⁴And they said, Thou hast not defrauded us, nor oppressed us, neither hast thou taken ought of any man's hand. ⁵And he said unto them, The LORD is witness against you, and his anointed is witness this day, that ye have not found ought in my hand. And they answered, He is witness.

Prophet Samuel's mother Hannah sacrificed time, resources, and pleasure to train Samuel to be a godly child. The fear and the love of God in Samuel were imparted to him at home by his mother Hannah during his foundational stage – ages 0-7. She said I will not go up until the child is weaned. This means to train a child to cease elementary dependency on the mother for breast milk and Activities of Daily Living (ADLs), and to cease childish habits. Hannah knew that she needed to perform her duty of training up her child before giving him to the Lord as she promised. 1Samuel 1:22 *"But Hannah went not up; for she said unto her husband, I will not go up until the child be weaned, and then I will bring him, that he may appear before the LORD, and there abide for ever."* She denied herself travel, even to the house of God just to devote time to training her son. She understood the importance of early childhood training. She knew that it would form the bedrock of Samuel's life. Because of this she was willing to sacrifice whatsoever it would take to lay a solid godly foundation for her son. In contrast, many Christian women in contemporary times will not sacrifice vacation, pleasure, work, time, and resources to raise a godly child for the Lord. Yet they wonder why their children are manifesting ungodly characters. Some go as far as blaming and questioning God. Rather, look inward, look at the mirror, and ask the woman in the mirror; did you really do your job as a mother in training up that child? Ask yourself am I really doing my job right now as a mother in training up my child? Ask yourself, have I really sacrificed all that is necessary to raise up a godly child for the LORD? You will not reap what you have not sown.

Hannah reaped the fruits of her labor. Samuel did not bring her shame but honor as it is today. Prophet Samuel did not depart from the path he was trained to follow all the days of his life. Evil was not found in him by God and by man, he did that which was right in the sight of God all through his ministry. Here is the conversation between Prophet Samuel and the children of Israel at the end of his ministry *"Behold, here I am: witness against me before the LORD, and before his anointed: whose ox have I taken? or whose ass have I taken? or whom have I defrauded? whom have I oppressed? or of whose hand have I received any bribe to blind mine eyes therewith? and I will restore it you. And they said, Thou hast not defrauded us, nor oppressed us, neither hast thou taken ought of any man's hand. And he said unto them, The LORD is witness against you, and his anointed is witness this day, that ye have not found ought in my hand. And they answered, He is witness."* This is the outcome of sacrificial labor in child training by a godly woman. Hannah honored God by taking heed to obey God's Word and God honored His Word in her life. Proverbs 22:6 *"Train up a child in the way he should go: and when he is old, he will not depart from it."* The good news is that it is not too late to make amends and do something. Woman! God is counting on you to raise Him godly children. May you find grace to accomplish this as you obey and take actions of faith in Jesus' name, Amen.

Pastor Timothy: 2Timothy 1:5; 3:14-15

1:5When I call to remembrance the unfeigned (genuine) faith that is in thee, which dwelt first in thy grandmother Lois, and thy mother Eunice; and I am persuaded that in thee also. 3:14But continue thou in the things which thou hast learned and hast been assured of, knowing of whom thou hast learned them; 3:15And that from a child thou hast known the holy scriptures, which are able to make thee wise unto salvation through faith which is in Christ Jesus.

The genuine faith and godly character Apostle Paul witnessed in the life of Pastor Timothy was imparted to him at childhood by his mother and grandmother. 2Timithy 3:15 *"And that from a child thou hast known the holy scriptures, which are able to make thee wise unto salvation through faith which is in Christ Jesus."* Why was not Timothy's grandfather and father credited for his godly life? It is because his godly character was imparted in him when he was a child at the foundational stage of ages 0-7; his mother and grandmother were the ones who weaned him. Naturally as God has ordained it, and also traditionally, a child is more attached to his mother for loving care, food, and warmth at this stage. Timothy's mother and grandmother did not waste his precious character-molding stage by pampering him and spoiling him with grandma's love. They sacrificed all that was necessary to raise a godly child for the LORD. Glory to God Almighty for a godly and disciplined grandmother who did not spoil her grandchild with ungodly love but dedicated time to training him in the fear of the LORD. It is also evident that it is Lois, Timothy's grandmother who trained up Eunice his mother to become the godly woman who also trained up a godly child for the LORD.

Mothers always receive credit and acknowledgement for a well-trained godly child as seen in the Scripture. God and man will always praise the mother for a godly child because mothers are naturally disposed to train the child within the character formative years. Consequentially the mother will always receive the blame from both God and man for an ungodly child. When King Saul thought that Jonathan his son was behaving foolishly. He quickly turned his anger on Jonathan's mother because he believed she had raised an unreasonable child for him.

Proverbs 10:1

The proverbs of Solomon. A wise son maketh a glad father: but a foolish son is the heaviness of his mother.

1 Samuel 20:30

Then Saul's anger was kindled against Jonathan, and he said unto him, Thou son of the perverse rebellious woman, do not I know that thou hast chosen the son of Jesse to thine own confusion, and unto the confusion of thy mother's nakedness?

The role of a mother in raising godly children for the LORD cannot be overemphasized. Ages zero to seven is the most important and effective period in child training – character molding wise. The impact of character training done at this stage is life-changing and life-lasting. At this stage, the child is not yet rigid, but tender and easy to mold. Women are naturally and traditionally positioned to exploit this opportunity. Failure to do so leaves a vacuum for Satan and his agents to exploit and kiddify the children. That is, turn them to stubborn and rebellious goat-like spirited hell-bound children of Satan. Mothers, and grandmothers; please make the optimum use of this period in raising up godly children for the LORD. God is counting on you. Honor God by taking heed to obey His Word in training up your child early, and God will honor His Word in your life and your family by keeping that child in His way all the days of his life. Proverbs 22:6, *"Train up a child in the way he should go: and when he is old, he will not depart from it."*

CHAPTER 3

Don't Kiddify Your Children

———————o———————

D on't Kiddify Your Children is a follow-up principle to *call them children and not Kids*. As we have seen so far, Satan's agenda is to make you 'Kiddify' your children in your thoughts and understanding, thereby making you believe that all they need to develop into functional adults is all the kiddy stuff he promotes through his various agents. All these are in his effort to lay the foundation of your children's lives and condition their minds to conform to his evil world's thought process. The Bible admonishes that we should not be conformed to this world.

Romans 12:2

And be not conformed to this world: but be ye transformed by the renewing of your mind, that ye may prove what is that good, and acceptable, and perfect, will of God.

"Be not" in this verse speaks of proactive and active measures to resist conformity to this world. This also implies that there are expected negative occurrences, maneuvers, deception, and proactive and active plans to get one to conform to this world. Satan is the ruler of this world's evil system and his goal is to get humanity to conform to his world system of thoughts. Since humans are governed by their thought processes, the end result is sinful habits and lifestyles.

For this reason, Satan has employed and deployed many mind-programming devices in the world to accomplish his task. These mind-programming devices include social media, music, TV, cartoons, video games, dolls, etc. Therefore, parents are deceived into leaving the most valuable period of training for their children in the hands of Satan through, social media, music, TV, cartoons, video games, and other 'kiddifying' Satanic devices like dolls, etc. Then through all his kiddifying devices, Satan ends up raising young kids and big kids for Christian parents. That is to say, young goats and big goats, Kiddified children—children who do not know the LORD nor care about the things of the LORD.

Hosea 5:5-7

⁵And the pride of Israel doth testify to his face: therefore shall Israel and Ephraim fall in their iniquity; Judah also shall fall with them. ⁶They shall go with their flocks and with their herds to seek the LORD; but they shall not find him; he hath withdrawn himself from them. ⁷They have dealt treacherously against the LORD: FOR THEY HAVE BEGOTTEN STRANGE CHILDREN: now shall a month devour them with their portions.

God was reproving the children of Israel for raising strange children for Him. One thing we should know about our God is that He is highly interested in children. That is why He said in Matthew 19:14, *"... Suffer little children, and forbid them not, to come unto me: for of such is the kingdom of heaven."*

The LORD is highly interested in godly offspring. When the Lord says He hates divorce, it is because He desires godly offspring. He desires godly children. So, when you abandon your children to TV, music, social media, video games, dolls, and other Satan's kiddifying devices. You have succeeded in handing over your children to Satan to train them. Subsequently, you have failed to observe God's commandment, which says you should train them to fear and honor Him.

Malachi 2:15-16

¹⁵And did not he make one? Yet had he the residue of the spirit. And wherefore one? THAT HE MIGHT SEEK A GODLY SEED. Therefore take heed to your spirit, and let none deal treacherously against the wife of his youth. ¹⁶For the LORD, the God of Israel, saith that he hateth putting away: for one covereth violence with his garment, saith the LORD of hosts: therefore take heed to your spirit, that ye deal not treacherously.

Genesis 18:19

For I know him, that he will command his children and his household after him, and they shall keep the way of the LORD, to do justice and judgment; that the LORD may bring upon Abraham that which he hath spoken of him.

God spoke confidently of Abraham that He knows he will raise his children in the way of the LORD. God said, "For I know him, that he will command his children..." This means that Abraham will stand his ground on godly training for his children, speaking boldly and authoritatively to ensure his children follow the way of the LORD. Training children requires time and resources; Abraham and Sarah must have sacrificed time and resources to accomplish this.

The children of Israel failed to train their children in the ways of the Lord. Their children could not come to the LORD because they were goats who were stubborn and rebellious and would not answer the call of the LORD. They raised children whom God could not recognize; strange children. How could this have happened? They abandoned their children in the hands of Satan in pursuit of wealth and the pleasures of the heathen nations.

Malachi 5:5-7

⁵And the pride of Israel doth testify to his face: therefore shall Israel and Ephraim fall in their iniquity; Judah also shall fall with them. ⁶They shall go with their flocks and with their herds to seek the LORD; but they shall not find him; he hath withdrawn himself from them. ⁷They have dealt treacherously against the LORD: for they have begotten strange children: now shall a month devour them with their portions.

Many parents have employed these Satan's kiddifying devices as their babysitters because they are too busy running after careers and dollars. When they are home, they are too tired and engaged with other things that need attention. Therefore, they rely on these kiddifying devices for babysitting. If you abandon your children to social media, music, TV, Cartoons, video games, dolls, and other Santan's kiddifying devices because you are busy running after things of minimal value compared to your children. You will end up with children who are estranged from the LORD. Kiddified children are children who do not fear the LORD nor care about the things of God. Children who hate the ways of the LORD.

3.1 Negative Effects of Worldly Music On Children

Music! Music! Music!!! I am referring to worldly music. There is no greater satanic programming and kiddifying agent than worldly music. One of the greatest, if not the greatest of all the devices of Satan in programming people's minds to conform to his desired worldview is music. This does not pertain to children alone but to people of all ages. Music activates almost every part of the brain from the limbic to the motor systems. Therefore, it increases blood flow to the region of the brain that generates emotions. It activates and keeps memories alive and drives the motor system to move the listener into action. This is why people are moved to dance, tap their hands, or nod their heads to the sound of music. The three major components of the effect of music on its listeners are Emotion, Memory Retention, and Action. Music activates the emotions of its listeners, helps them to remember the message, and moves them to action. Music could be a great asset that can be used to positively shape a person's character when the message of the music is good, rational, and positive.

This is why some of the Word of God in the Bible are given to us in Psalms and songs. God inspired Moses to compose a song about the victory God gave them at the Red Sea over the Egyptians so they never forget, Exodus chapter 15. Also, shortly before God asked Moses to go to Mount Abarim to die, He gave Moses a very important message for the children of Israel as a song so that they would not forget it; Deuteronomy

32. I remember struggling with the spelling of correction as a child and my mother spelled it for me in a song format, and from that day forward it never departed from me. This was why King Lemuel's mother gave him the most important lessons for his life and success in a song format. His mother gave him the lesson as a song to stir up his emotions and cause him to always remember the lessons, in order to move him to take the right actions in life. It is difficult to forget a message given as a song because as the receiver repeats the song, the message is engraved in his or her subconscious mind and ultimately shapes his or her character and worldview.

King Lemuel: Proverbs 31:1-5

¹The words of king Lemuel, the prophecy that his mother taught him. ²What, my son? and what, the son of my womb? and what, the son of my vows? ³Give not thy strength unto women, nor thy ways to that which destroyeth kings. ⁴It is not for kings, O Lemuel, it is not for kings to drink wine; nor for princes strong drink: ⁵Lest they drink, and forget the law, and pervert the judgment of any of the afflicted.

In the eighteenth century, Andrew Fletcher of Scotland said *"Let me make the songs of a nation, and I care not who makes its laws"* There is a great insight into the effect of music on its listeners in this saying. This does not imply that laws are not important, of course, one will either be justified or condemned by the law whether the laws of God or those of nations. This saying reveals the fact that the person who controls the music of a nation controls the people's character and determines the culture of the land. The three major components of the effect of music on its listeners are Emotion, Memory Retention, and

Action. Music activates the emotions of its listeners, helps them to remember and retain the message, and moves them to action. The message of the music is easily engraved in the listener's subconscious mind through the arousal of emotion (passion) and repetition. This ultimately shapes the person's worldview and character. Unfortunately, this great tool of character molding called music is in the very hands of Satan. Satan is highly skilled in music and he is the inspiration behind worldly music. His goal is to shape and control the character and culture of the nations to the eternal damnation of their souls in hell.

Isaiah 14:10-12

[10]They all shall speak and say to you: 'Have you also become as weak as we? Have you become like us? [11]Your pomp is brought down to Sheol, AND THE SOUND OF YOUR STRINGED INSTRUMENTS; The maggot is spread under you, And worms cover you.' [12]"How you are fallen from heaven, O Lucifer, son of the morning! How you are cut down to the ground, You who weakened the nations! (NKJV)

The Bible verses above speak of the fall and the impending eternal judgment in hell of Lucifer a.k.a Satan and the Devil. His musical skills are referenced in verse 11, *"and the sound of your stringed instruments."* Note, "instruments" with the "s" Satan is the master musician diversely skilled in all types of musical instruments. He is the master instrumentalist creating and inspiring the lyrics and melodies of worldly music. His goal is to mold the character and culture of the nations to the damnation of the people's souls in hellfire.

Before becoming a Christian, the strongest influence that shaped my ungodly philosophies and characters was music; hip hop/rap music in particular, especially the songs of Snoop Dogg. One of those Snoop Dogg's songs that really altered my character for the worse was Gin and Juice. Here is a sample of the lyrics *"Keep rolling down the streets smoking indo (marijuana) sipping on gin and juice; laid back, with my mind on my money and my money on my mind."* Is this not a message inspired by Satan from hell? This lyrics sample of Snoop Dogg's "Gin and Juice" is saintly compared to some other lyrics especially those of current hip hop/rap music. Snoop Dogg's Gin and Juice song changed my view on marijuana, alcohol, and money. As I continuously played and sang the song, the message was engraved in my subconscious mind and ultimately shaped my character. I started to consume marijuana and gin and juice and made money my god. All glory to God Almighty; my LORD and Savior Jesus Christ who delivered me from the grip of Satan.

Although the Bible condemned and characterized the nature of dogs as ungodly and evil. Notwithstanding, Satan through the power and influence of worldly music was able to inspire and influence children to call themselves dogs and behave like dogs. God will never call His children dogs and will not be pleased with humans He created in His image calling themselves dogs or manifesting the characteristics of a dog. God does not hate dogs, and dogs are good animals because God said that everything He created is very good and this includes dogs; Genesis 1:31. However, God detests any human being that manifests the nature and character of a dog because it is evil for humans to behave like dogs.

Proverbs 26:11

As a dog returneth to his vomit, so a fool returneth to his folly.

Matthew 7:6

Give not that which is holy unto the dogs, neither cast ye your pearls before swine, lest they trample them under their feet, and turn again and rend you.

Philippians 3:2

Beware of dogs, beware of evil workers, beware of the concision.

Revelation 22:15

For without are dogs, and sorcerers, and whoremongers, and murderers, and idolaters, and whosoever loveth and maketh a lie.

God detests those that manifest the nature and characteristics of dogs, and they have no place in His kingdom. However, Satan has rewritten the negativity about the characteristics of a dog in our time through worldly music. This we can see in the hip-hop/rap music world, where young people happily proclaim and celebrate that they are dogs. The artists and their followers openly proclaim that they are dogs, they put on dogs' chains and doggy pendants of all kinds. Satan inspired rap artists to use doggy stage names like Doggy Fresh, Snoop Dogg, Dog Pound, Lil Bow Wow, Pitbull, etc. They have glamorized and glorified the characteristics of a dog as a human lifestyle; a thing which God hates. When children continuously listen to and sing these songs, the message will be engraved in their subconscious mind and will ultimately shape their character. What are the characteristics of dogs? Violence, Dominance, Promiscuity, and living just for pleasure.

Through worldly music demonic spirits infest the human mind and body to manifest the characteristics of dogs. The more these singers and their listeners/fans confess that they are dogs, the more they invoke the demonic doggy spirit in them, taking them deeper and deeper into sin. Thereby alienating them further away from God and aligning them with hell and Satan. This is why there is so much sexual promiscuity and violence among these dog-glamorizing hip-hop/rap artists and their fans. It is absolutely normal and entertaining for them to engage in reckless sexual lifestyles with multiple partners. They unashamedly glamorize and glorify their doggy lifestyles through music. Music activates and keeps memories alive and drives the motor system to move the listener into action. This is why you find little girls twerking (sexually provoking dance) and ten-year-old girls getting pregnant; Kiddified children. This is why there is so much sexual promiscuity and violence in the hip-hop community, after all, dogs sleep around and fight each other "Dog eat Dog". They behave like dogs because the doggy demonic spirits have taken over them through the power and influence of worldly music. Andrew Fletcher: *"Let me make the songs of a nation, and I care not who makes its laws"* The person who controls the music of a nation controls the people's character and determines the culture of the land. The one obviously controlling the music of the nations is Satan. Christian parents who desire to raise godly children must shield their children from getting Kiddified through worldly music.

3.2 Negative Effects of TV And Cartoons on Children

There are several TV shows and cartoons that encourage ungodly behaviors in children. They give ungodly messages to children. They contain sexual innuendos, and sexual scenes, encourage aggression, and promote stubbornness and rebellious behavior in children. These TV shows and cartoons affect children's behavior and make them think it is normal to be aggressive, spoiled, stubborn, rebellious, violent, and sexually immoral.

According to AACAP (American Academy of Child and Adolescent Psychiatry), *"Children who view shows in which violence is very realistic, frequently repeated, or unpunished are more likely to imitate what they see. The child's brain and eyes are usually affected by the speed of the images affects."* According to their research, shows with high-speed image affects, in which violence is very realistic, frequently repeated, or unpunished destroy children's character, brain, and eyes. According to AACAP, children who view such shows are more likely to imitate what they see. It is the same God-given natural principle in training a child that is at play. ***Proverbs 22:6, "Train up a child in the way he should go: and when he is old, he will not depart from it."***

Early Years Psychology says, "Give me the child until he is seven and I will make him what you want him to be." This psychology says ages 0-7 are the formative years of a child; that is, character molding-wise. Everything else we do after age zero to seven to mold the character of a child cannot be foundational and may not last. The philosophy is, "The earlier the better." It is the same God-given natural principle of training a child that is at work here. Proverbs 22:6, ***"Train up*** *a child in the way he should go: and when he is old, he will not depart from it."* Satan knows that the children will not depart from his desired lifestyle if he succeeds in shaping them in knowledge and character at the foundational stage – Ground-Zero, (age 0-7). The world and Satan understand this God-given natural principle and take due advantage of it. This is why Satan deceived parents to believe that all their children needed to grow and mature are these kiddifying devices so you could abandon your children to him.

While AACAP is more focused on violence and the physical defects caused by TV shows and cartoons. Heavenly-minded Christian parents should also be concerned about the spiritual effects of these TV shows and cartoons on their children. What other ungodly behaviors have you observed in TV shows, and cartoons that are very realistic, frequently repeated, and unpunished? Make your list…. tantrum, lying, stealing, stubbornness, rebellion, vulgar language, gay, lesbianism, genderfluidity, transgenderism, sexual acts and sexual innuendos, etc.

Your Children will imitate these ungodly characters and much more if you abandon them to TV shows and cartoons. These characters will form the foundation of their lives and they will most likely not depart from them. TV shows and cartoons are Satan's mind-programming devices in the world to accomplish his task of raising children that are alienated from God. If you leave the most valuable period of training your children in the hands of Satan through TV shows, and cartoons. Satan will succeed in raising young goats and big goats for you, Kiddified children—children who do not know the LORD nor care about the things of the LORD.

3.3 Negative Effects of Video Games on Children

Video games have all the negative effects of cartoons and an addictive tendency which affects the intellectual development of children. Video games are cartoons 2.0; they are cartoons on steroids. This is so because the children now assume the character role in the cartoon, they are playing the character roles themselves. This makes video gaming more addictive and damaging to children. The high-speed image affects, glorified violent acts, and sexual acts in most of these video games are on steroids. Then you could only imagine how damaging they are to children knowing that they now impersonate those characters. When a child is playing any video game, he or she impersonates the character in the game; the child becomes that character. It becomes very personal for the child and ultimately affects his thinking and character. This is why video gaming is very addictive and a child would do anything, give up, and abandon whatever just to spend endless time playing video games.

I fully understand the addictive and damaging effects of video games on children even when it is seemingly harmless games like sports and so on. I know this because I witnessed it for myself while in secondary school and while doing business in Nigeria. During my secondary school days in Ikeja, Nigeria. Students will leave school during school hours to Allen Avenue also in Ikeja to play video games. Most of these students will steal their parents' money in thousands and will waste it all playing video games. Some will steal their parents' properties like jewelry, electronics, and whatever is of value, sell them, and waste the money on gaming and other things. Some of the games they played were violent while some were just regular nonviolent games. Nonetheless, the effect on them was all the same. It was addictive and the children would do anything, give up, and abandon whatever just to spend endless time playing video games. They stole their parents' money and properties, abandoned classes, and risked the consequences of their theft, and of abandoning school, if or when they got caught. Most of these students did not as well do well in school as they ought to have done. They wasted class time, study time, and homework time playing video games.

I witnessed this game joint where these students usually go to play games make millions from these children. I knew this because I had been to the game joint on one or two occasions and also from students talking about the games they played and how much money they spent playing games. I also know this because I later got to know the person who managed that game joint after I started my own business. We became friends and talked about how much money they used to make from the game joint when he was the manager. Being naturally business-minded minded I knew that there was a lot of money to be made in gaming right from my secondary school days. I knew because the victims are addicted and are willing to part with any amount just to get their high and next high.

Knowing that there is a lot of money to make in the gaming business, I delved into it after secondary school. I was not disappointed; I made a lot of money. It was through the gaming business that I made enough money to start traveling abroad to import game consoles like Sony PlayStation, and Super Nintendo and their accessories. I witnessed children sit in my gaming joint from morning to evening/night playing games. When their money finishes, they will quickly go home and return with more money. They would steal their parents' money and spend it at my game joint. They wasted most of their day at my game joint and were not very useful to their parents nor had time to do things that would add value to their lives, like studying. I did not care then because I did not know any better, all I wanted was to make money. Knowing what I know now I would never have gone into such an ungodly business. These children were behaving like drug addicts. They would spend their money for food on games at my joint. They stole their parents' money and properties, abandoned classes, and risked the consequences just to get their high and next high in gaming.

3.4 Negative Effects of Dolls on Children

The eyes are a gateway to a person's life. Whatever goes in through the eyes ultimately shapes a person's character and lifestyle. This is a natural principle. Whatever goes in through the eyes gateway has the potential to shape one's life through the thought process. What people see are processed through thoughts to form opinions that may settle in the heart and shape one's character and perspective on life. Jacob understood this principle of life and used this powerful tool to convert almost all of Laban's flocks to become his.

Jacob has been serving Laban his father-in-law for many years and Laban has been changing their agreement just to keep Jacob serving him perpetually. After Jacob's wife gave birth to Joseph, he asked Laban to send him away to start his own life with his family. However, Laban wanted to convince Jacob to continue to stay and serve him because he knew that God was blessing him because of Jacob. He asked Jacob to name his wages in order to stay and continue serving him. Jacob suggested that he let him keep all the flocks that were brown, speckled, and spotted among the sheep, goats, and cattle as his wages. Laban quickly grabbed this deal because these colors are not usually common among the flocks. Laban knew that all things being equal, it was a wonderful deal for him as Jacob would only end up getting very little flocks as his wages. He never knew that Jacob had a game plan that had been proven to be very successful.

Genesis 30:37-43

[30]And Jacob took him rods of green poplar, and of the hazel and chesnut tree; and pilled white strakes in them, and made the white appear which was in the rods. [38]And he set the rods which he had pilled before the flocks in the gutters in the watering troughs when the flocks came to drink, that they should conceive when they came to drink [39]And the flocks conceived before the rods, and brought forth cattle ringstraked, speckled, and spotted. [40]And Jacob did separate the lambs, and set the faces of the flocks toward the ringstraked, and all the brown in the flock of Laban; and he put his own flocks by themselves, and put them not unto Laban's cattle. [41]And it came to pass, whensoever the stronger cattle did conceive, that Jacob laid the rods before the eyes of the cattle in the gutters, that they might conceive among the rods. [42]But when the cattle were feeble, he put them not in: so the feebler were Laban's, and the stronger Jacob's. [43]And the man increased exceedingly, and had much cattle, and maidservants, and menservants, and camels, and asses.

Jacob took rods of green poplar, hazel, and chestnut trees and peeled white strips in them to create ringstraked, speckled, and spotted rods. He would then place these rods before the flocks in the watering throughs where the flocks came to drink water. As the flocks constantly see these rods as they drink water and conceive, it passes a coded message to design the baby that is being formed in the womb. Because the eyes are a gateway these coded messages that their eyes constantly send internally are being decoded and processed as beauty and sent to design the forming baby in the womb. Therefore, when the flocks give birth; their offspring are ringstraked, speckled, and spotted. Jacob used this natural principle to convert almost all of Laban's flocks to his own.

Many people are familiar with the saying "You are what eat" and few are familiar with "You are what you hear" but most people are not familiar with "You are what you see." These sayings are true because the mouth, ears, and eyes are gateways to a person's life. Whatever goes into a person through the mouth, ears, and eyes has the potential to shape the outcome of that person's life. Jacob exploited the eyes gateway and succeeded in converting most of Laban's flocks to become his. Satan has also exploited, and still exploiting the eyes gateway, and has succeeded and still succeeding in converting most of God's creation to become his.

Have you ever wondered how it became possible for a rational mind to fix fake eyelashes, and think it made her beautiful? If you were told twenty years ago that normal human beings would buy fake eyelashes with their money and glue them to their eyes for beauty, would you have believed? How did women arrive at this debased mindset of believing that gluing fake eyelashes to their eyes and dying their hair to strange hair colors is a rational act of beautification? Have you ever wondered how the human mind got so debased to see a half-naked lady to be hot and beautiful instead of shameful? Have you ever wondered why women gravitate towards adding everything artificial to a natural body from makeup to fake hair, fake nails, etc., and think it is beautiful? Have you ever wondered how a supposedly rational mind arrived at dying his/her hair pink, purple, yellow, green, red etc., and sees it as beautiful? You really do not have to think for long or look very far to find the answers. It all started with the dolls.

Just like Jacob; Satan engineered the creation of dolls with these naturally unrealistic beauty features like very large eyelashes. Painted their nails and dressed them half naked. Then with the help of parents, he positioned them before the children continually. Satan had positioned these images before the children from their infancy as the image of beauty just like

Jacob positioned the ringstraked, speckled, and spotted rods before Laban's flocks, and they caused Laban's flocks to birth ringstraked, speckled, and spotted offspring. In the same way, has Satan positioned these dolls before God's creation and caused God's children to raise strange children for the LORD. Malachi 5:7, *"They have dealt treacherously against the LORD: for they have begotten strange children: now shall a month devour them with their portions."* As the children constantly behold, admire, and play with these dolls, coded messages are transmitted into their senses through the eyes' gateway. Therefore, these messages are then decoded by the child's brain to mean; "This is the standard of beauty, this is what is called beautiful, you must look like this to be called beautiful." The child is being trained non-verbally in their foundational stage through these doll images. The child internalizes all that he or she is receiving and it forms the foundation of his or her life which the child will not depart from except for a divine intervention. Proverbs 22:6, *"Train up a child in the way he should go: and when he is old, he will not depart from it."*

When the female child grows up, it is already laid in her on the foundational level that putting on everything artificial and dressing half-naked is the standard of beauty, and that she must look like that to be called beautiful. While the males are wired at their foundational stage to only appreciate, admire, lust after and compliment females who are dressed half-naked and are artificially made-up. And which woman does not want to be called beautiful? She will absolutely see nothing wrong with dressing as such and the sense of it being shameful and embarrassing will not be there at all. Therefore, when she goes to the store, she is looking for the clothing that will make her beautiful by the standard she was trained through these satanic dolls. When Satan later on down the road introduces fake eyelashes, she would have no problem jumping at them because they fit her perfect description of beauty as she observed in these dolls growing up. What the children have been seeing and admiring in these dolls has gone through their thought process to form opinions and shape their perspective in life on beauty. It has set their standard for beauty and acceptable clothing. Parents who truly want to raise godly children must guard their children from beholding images that will destroy their moral foundations and this includes these ungodly dolls.

3.5 Demonic Possession Through Cartoons, Video Games, and Dolls

Since the emergence of cartoon films over a century ago, several generations of children have grown up watching animated movies. Many girls have fantasized about being princesses and many boys have imagined themselves to be valiant knights after watching cartoons like Peter Pan, Aladdin and the Magic Lamp, Cinderella, Beauty and the Beast, etc. Why do children want to become these cartoon characters and why do they manifest the ungodly behaviors of these cartoon and video game characters?

Most of these cartoons and video game characters are facsimiles of demonic spirits. This is why you find that in recent times, cartoon characters have become monstrous and are all kinds of creepy and scary creatures. Have you ever wondered why the sudden change of cartoon characters to monstrous images; are scary images the best appeal to children? Satan has been animating demons, giving them charming and charismatic characters and presenting them to children as adorable heroes. These demonic spirits present themselves as heroes with loving and charming charismatic characters worthy of idolizing.

2Corinthians 11:14-15

¹⁴And no marvel; for Satan himself is transformed into an angel of light. ¹⁵Therefore it is no great thing if his ministers also be transformed as the ministers of righteousness; whose end shall be according to their works.

Satan is very subtle; deception and manipulation are his strongest weapons to kill, steal, and destroy as recorded in **John 10:10.** Demons are his ministers. They are his ministering spirits. He has transformed many of his demons into ministers of righteousness to deceive Christians through false revelations. In the same way, Satan has also transformed these demons into animated heroes of charming and adorable charismatic characters to deceive children. Most of these cartoon characters including the good-looking and the monstrous ones are facsimiles of demonic spirits. This is evident by the ungodly character and attitude they display and glamorize to the children. Character such as bratty behavior, lying, tantrums, stubbornness, rebellion, violence, immoral sexual behaviors, etc. The children are deceived and they fall in love with these demonic replicas and deem them friendly. Then they start to idolize and imitate the characters of these demonic animated characters.

The children are desensitized from fearing these would have been scary images because of their heroic and charming characters. These demonic spirits then appear to the children in the dream as their familiar dolls, cartoons, and game characters to possess them. Now, because the children have been desensitized and deceived to see them as friendly and charismatic, they will not be alarmed. The children will freely embrace and interact with them and these demons will enter them and they become possessed. This is why you see some children uncontrollably manifest some of these ungodly characteristics like tantrums, lying, stubbornness, rebellion, sexual immorality, anger, violence, etc. at levels beyond human comprehension. You would have also observed that every effort made to help and change children like this is usually fruitless. This is because the matter has gone beyond the physical; the matter is spiritual and only Jesus can deliver them.

It is satanic manipulation and deception to make parents think that their children would not have a normal childhood and grow into responsible functional adults without these dolls and other kiddifying devices. I always want to examine matters from the empirical standpoint; that is, from the point of experience and observations. Many generations grew up without these Satan's kiddifying devices. Could anyone say that they did not have a normal childhood, or say that they did not become responsible and functional adults? You may not have grown up with these kiddifying devices. Would you claim to be dysfunctional in life because you were not raised with these things? Could anyone say that the generations that grew up without these kiddifying devices are more morally bankrupt? The answers to these questions are obvious. On the contrary, it is the generation that grew up with these satanic kiddifying agents that are more morally bankrupt and dysfunctional because they were Kiddified.

Don't 'Kiddify' your children, is simply saying; don't hand over your children to Satan through his kiddifying devices like TV, social media, music, cartoons, dolls, video games, and other Satanic kiddifying devices. Satan is a goat-like spirited being, filled with rebellion and stubbornness towards God. This is why the image of Satan is represented by a goat-like creature; the Baphomet image. If you leave your children in his hands, he will raise them up goat-like spirited children in his likeness. Children that have been Kiddified; who are filled with rebellion, stubbornness, and all manner of sinfulness. Children who will not come to the LORD nor obey Him. Children whom the LORD will not recognize, who will end up with their father Satan in hell fire for all eternity.

Matthew 25:33-34, 41

[33]And he shall set the sheep on his right hand, but the goats on the left. [34]Then shall the King say unto them on his right hand, Come, ye blessed of my Father, inherit the kingdom prepared for you from the foundation of the world: [41]Then shall he say also unto them on the left hand, Depart from me, ye cursed, into everlasting fire, prepared for the devil and his angels:

3.6 Recommendations and Alternatives to Cartoons, Video Games and Dolls

All that has been discussed previously is not to say that one should not buy any type of toy, doll, or video game or allow their children to watch any type of cartoon. All that I have pointed out is that the devil uses these things to devise mischief for the children. Also, these things are unnecessary to raise a child to become a moral and functional adult. Therefore, parents must exercise knowledge, wisdom, and great caution when buying any and what they allow their children to watch. Christian parents must guard against Satan from kiddifying their children with these devices. That is to say; guard against Satan from turning your children into spiritual goats through cartoons, video games, and dolls. This being said, the most important thing is that they should not become an alternative to parenting. They should not replace parental roles in the children's life. They must not take the most important part of your children's life. Parents must sacrifice time to be there to nurture and train their children if they truly want to raise godly children. They must transform their children's lives with the Word of God.

Romans 12:2

And be not conformed to this world: but be ye transformed by the renewing of your mind, that ye may prove what is that good, and acceptable, and perfect, will of God.

Christian parents should devise fun ways to keep their children busy with the Word of God and should be involved. This will keep the children from conforming to the ways of the world and the desires of the world. This is why Romans 12:2 further admonishes us to become transformed from this world's system of thought and sinful lifestyles by renewing our minds with the Word of God. This will invariably produce the heavenly system of thoughts that will produce the desired godly lifestyle.

Recommendations:

1. Parents should not use cartoons and video games as their babysitters.

2. Parents should avoid all cartoons and video games for entertainment if possible.

3. Avoid educational cartoons where possible and use children's educational videos taught by actual humans.

4. Allow only appropriate educational cartoons where necessary if inevitable.

5. Limit the time spent watching inevitable necessary educational cartoons.

6. Parents should watch TV/cartoons with their children and always take time to explain the difference between cartoons and reality as the need arises.

7. Parents should not allow their children to eat with the TV or iPad on.

8. Parents should not leave their children with TV or iPad alone for long without monitoring them.

Alternatives to Cartoons and Video Games:

1. Children love outside games (Jump rope, running, soccer, etc.) children will forget that TV, iPads, Phones,

and dolls exist once they are outside. The problem is that most parents have sold and enslaved themselves to dollars. Therefore, they have no time to sacrifice for their children to do the things that children actually love doing. Most of these devices are usually relevant only when children cannot go out to play.

2. Instead of going to the gym and spending unnecessary money. Turn your workout time to time with the children outside. Engaging with the children in outside games will burn the calories needed and simultaneously create quality time with the children, eliminating the need for any kiddifying device.

3. Create Bible story time and have your children tell the Bible stories and the family can ask them questions. This presupposes that parents have already created the environment for their children to learn the Bible. Otherwise, how could they be able to tell Bible stories? Christian parents must teach their children the Word of God that is able to transform them.

4. Organize family Bible quizzes with rewards. Set a long-term prize reward like quarterly, six months, and yearly, and keep records of scores to build up for the prizes. Please let the prizes or rewards not be the same things you are trying to get them away from (iPads, games, phones, dolls, etc.)

5. **Your turn to add to the list...**

KIDDIFIED is a prelude to the book "The Principles of Raising Godly Children." Kiddified covered three chapters out of the ten chapters of The Principles of Raising Godly Children. If you desire to raise godly children or knows Christian parents you desire that they raise godly children for the LORD. Then you should recommend or get them a copy of ***The Principles of Raising Godly Children (Coming Soon in Six Months from the published date of KIDDIFIED)***

OTHER BOOKS WRITTEN BY THE AUTHOR

1 TRUMP THE GREAT! THE 45TH & 47TH PRESIDENT OF THE UNITED STATES. GOD'S END-TIME VESSEL

Amazon Book Reviews On Trump The Great!

1. ngel59: Second coming of Christ

This book opened my eyes to how close our lord Jesus is coming soon. The current events are just the beginning of what's to come.

2 Lala: Very Insightful, Second Coming Of Jesus Christ!

Just finished this book, great read!

The storytelling, insight, humor, humility, and scriptural relations in the writing are remarkable. The style of writing is engaging, I love the way the book ended, the very last page.

We choose you, President Donald J Trump!

TRUMPITO we stand with you! Much love from New Jersey! #MAGA #TRUMPFOREVERYONE

WHEN JESUS SAYS YES NOBODY CAN SAY NO!

THE KINGDOM OF GOD IS AT HAND, REPENT AND WALK WITH THE LORD IN HOLINESS AND RIGHTEOUSNESS TODAY!

3 Kindle Customer: The expectations of the righteous shall not be cut off

This is a striking representation and cover. The title says it all. God is truly at work, and anyone who knows that there is a creator and men are the creatures should venture to read this book. A well-thought-out book that flows with the sequence.

4. OG: Wow!

This indeed is the revelation of God to His children. Never in my years of reading the Bible have I understood the extract of scriptures sighted in this book; the 7 days of creation and its relation to the time of Christ coming. I am baffled at the author's understanding of the scripture and I am convinced that this is the Lord's doing. Indeed, He revealed secret things to them that fear Him. This is a strong wake-up call to me and Christians who await the rapture. It is all a cry unto sinners to come to Christ. I am blessed beyond words! I started this book as I woke up this morning because I had the burden to read it since yesterday for what reason, I don't know but now I know. I started reading this book and never dropped it till I finished it, I never wanted it to finish. This is a great evangelism tool. God bless the author, Pastor Cliff McAnthony. More grace! Maranatha!

5. Roxen Herman: A Must Read!

Very insightful and scripturally accurate. I highly recommend purchasing this book, you won't be disappointed.

2 THE STORY OF JESUS COLORING BOOK

Amazon Book Reviews on The Story of Jesus Coloring Book.

1 Chidu: Buy it and enjoy it

Children and adults alike would enjoy the simple easy to follow truth of God's word.

www.ingramcontent.com/pod-product-compliance
Lightning Source LLC
Chambersburg PA
CBHW060336130626
46553CB00003B/1017